RIPON MARKET PLACE

The evolution of the centre of a historic Yorkshire market town

Editor
Mike Younge

ISBN No 1 872618 20 0

Published by
Ripon Historical Society
and Ripon, Harrogate and District
Family History Group

Designed and printed by
Maxiprint,
York, England

CONTENTS

LIST OF ILLUSTRATIONS

FOREWORD

Various local publications over many years have dealt with Ripon's Cathedral and other important buildings in the town, but to date there has been no detailed study of its impressive Market Place, despite the vital part it has played in the town's life down the centuries.

There the people of Ripon have gathered for their food, drink, work and entertainment, especially on market days, whilst in the last hundred years this spacious area has become a major visitor attraction, providing the setting for Ripon's special nightly Hornblowing ceremony.

Ripon Historical Society decided therefore to mark the new Millennium by producing a history of the Market Place, tracing its evolution over eight centuries and commemorating its long term importance to the social and economic life of the town. In this book, general articles deal with the history of the Square as a whole, while more specific articles trace the story of the individual properties around it - in so far as the source material permits. A sad but inescapable fact is that precious little information survives for the first four hundred years of the Square's existence, from the 12th to the 16th centuries. It is only in the 17thC that a number of Market Place residents and their properties can first be clearly identified. One would dearly love to know more, for example, about such shadowy figures as Aunger de Frere, a cloth merchant who operated somewhere on the Market Place in the 14thC.

2001 is in fact a very suitable year to assess the historic importance of the Market Place, since quite fortuitously the first comprehensive refurbishment of the Square in its history has begun. Made possible by a massive Heritage Lottery grant coupled with substantial funding from both Harrogate Borough Council and North Yorkshire County Council, the refurbishment should leave the Square in fine fettle to face the next millennium.

Mike Younge
Editor.
May 2001

SOURCES

Two very different types of sources were required for this study, those needed for the public space and those for the properties surrounding it. Medieval sources are scanty for both categories and often reference has to be made to the layout of streets and properties, and comparison with similar manorial towns.

The situation begins to improve for both categories in the 17thC. For the public space the Corporation records are available although, since they take for granted contemporary knowledge, they can be frustrating. From the later 19thC, newspaper accounts supplement these. Much of the material has been collected in that monumental work the 'Ripon Millenary 1886' and has subsequently been extended, mainly from the newspapers, by 'A Ripon Record 1886-1986'.

The same sources can provide some material for the surrounding properties sometimes in the shape of details of the occupations and careers of property owners, and this can be supplemented by the Hearth Tax record of 1672 and the occasional sale catalogue, magazine article or architectural survey, but the basic material has never before been seriously examined.

The obvious first recourse was to investigate title deeds in the hands of the present owners. Some owners were immensely cooperative, but even where all the help possible was given there were only a few who had sets of title deeds which went back more than a century and a half, whereas we hoped to cover at least three centuries. One reason for this was discovered in the Vyner MSS in the Leeds Archives where there are more than 20 bundles of deeds of Market Place properties acquired by the Studley Estate in the 18th and early 19thC. When the Studley owners sold these properties they retained the old deeds.

Where the actual deeds were unavailable recourse could be had to the West Riding Registry of Deeds at Wakefield where Ripon deeds were registered from 1704 to 1970. This Registry is now part of the West Yorkshire Archives. Where property changed hands by inheritance and not by sale the probate records for the province of York until 1856 could be consulted at the Borthwick Institute, and Ripon parish registers.

But for all these records, except of course the current deeds, at least a full name of a previous owner was needed and these were provided by three street-by-street property surveys, those of 1675, 1747 and 1800.

The first of these only dealt with one type of property, the burgages which carried with them special rights, but since a good many of the Market Place properties were such burgages this was no real problem. The survey was made to check the rights of those who claimed ownership, and was the result of the displeasure of the Lord of the Manor, the Archbishop of York, at a show of independence by the burgesses in choosing a new MP for the borough without consulting his wishes.

The Average Award of 1747 was necessitated by the decision to free the owners of lands in the common fields of the grazing rights of others over their land. The reason for the making of John Humphries' survey of 1800 with its invaluable map is not known, but it may have been at the behest of the Studley estate. These three surveys provide the names of the owners of Ripon properties at the time they were made and have been invaluable in discovering which deeds or wills to investigate in Leeds, Wakefield and York.

Jean Denton

ACKNOWLEDGEMENTS

Thanks are due to all those writers who have contributed to this book, either through general articles or by researching the history of an individual property. Particular thanks are due to Chief Researcher Jean Denton who has contributed so much. Sadly two of the authors, Dr Bill Petchey and Geoff Hayward, died during the preparation of the book.

The documentary sources used are set out in a previous section, but special mention must be made of the assistance provided by the Leeds Archives office at Sheepscar and the Registry of Deeds at Wakefield where so much of the relevant material is held. Much help has also been received from the staff of the Ripon Campus College Library and from the owners and occupiers of the Market Place properties themselves.

For the provision of the illustrations, thanks are due to Ripon City Council, the Yorkshire Film Archive, and Ripon Local Studies Research Centre. Douglas Atkinson must be thanked for making his unique collection of early photographs available, and individual images have also been kindly provided by Keith Snowden, Stephen McKay and Michael Hutchinson.

Brian Carroll of Ripon Civic Society has produced the excellent map, and Crossley Eccles the fine watercolour that adorns the outer cover.

INTRODUCTION

For the benefit of readers unfamiliar with the story of Ripon, and to enable the history of the Market Place to be set in a wider context, a short account of Ripon's past is given below.

By the late 7thC Ripon had come into being as an Anglo-Saxon farming community settled around a monastery, famed for its turbulent and much-travelled leader Abbot Wilfrid. The crypt of the church which he dedicated in 672 still survives beneath the present Cathedral.

At the time of the Norman conquest the monastery had gone, replaced by a collegiate church controlled by the Archbishops of York, who were responsible for its periodic rebuilding in imposing style throughout the Middle Ages.

In the early medieval period the Archbishops of York were however also responsible for changing the whole face of Ripon - by creating a brand new town centre well to the west of the early church, and this Norman borough with its spacious market place was soon bringing the Archbishop a substantial income from its rents and tolls. The medieval street pattern which Ripon then acquired has survived largely unchanged to the present day.

Despite Scottish raids in the 14thC, Ripon headed by its Wakeman flourished in the late Middle Ages as a centre of cloth-making and as a place of pilgrimage for those seeking the shrine of St. Wilfrid, but with the Reformation in the 16thC the shrine was closed and clashes took place between Catholics and Protestants. In 1568 the Catholic Mary Queen of Scots stayed briefly in Ripon on her journey southwards. Her son James I showed Ripon special favour, granting important charters in 1604 to both church and town, and visiting Ripon in person in 1617. By then spur-making had become the town's most famous industry, and the king was duly presented with a silver set.

Ripon escaped the Civil War without major incident or serious damage, but by the end of the 17thC power and influence in the town was passing from the Archbishops of York to the wealthy Aislabie family of nearby Studley Royal. Whilst Mayor, John Aislabie contributed generously to the building of the Obelisk (1702) which has since become such a distinctive feature of the Square and where the Hornblower still Sets the nightly Watch.

During the 18thC the town centre underwent great visual change as nearly all the timber-framed black-and-white buildings were replaced (or just recased) in Georgian brick, the Wakeman's house being one of the few to survive relatively unchanged. It was at this time that the Square began to take on its present day appearance.

Despite the coming of the canal, long-distance stage-coaching services, and later the railway, Ripon remained basically a small market town with regular livestock fairs serving a farming area. In 1836 however its importance was dramatically enchanced when the great collegiate church was chosen to become the seat of the new Diocese of Ripon, its boundaries drawn to include the fast-growing industrial city of Leeds.

The 19thC as elsewhere saw rapid population growth, more housing, more churches and chapels, more industry, and improvements to public health. Ripon gained a new hospital, workhouse, prison, racecourse and teacher-training college, whilst the ancient grammar school was rebuilt on a more spacious site on the edge of the town. A new clock tower commemorated Queen Victoria's Diamond Jubilee, and a whole series of festivals began a tradition extending to the present day.

In Edwardian times Ripon tried with little success to emulate Harrogate as a spa town, but newcomers were soon to come in their thousands as a vast army camp was built on the western outskirts of the town during the First World War. Ripon saw many servicemen again during the Second World War, this time from the Royal Engineers base and from local airfields in the Vale of York.

In 1974 control of the town's affairs passed to Harrogate Borough Council and North Yorkshire County Council, but Ripon's proud status as a city was confirmed by special royal charter.

Further important changes came during the late 20thC with the coming of new light industry, more housing, new schools and eventually a bypass. The railway closed but the canal re-opened. Like historic towns elsewhere, however, Ripon came to need and value its tourists, as it did the pilgrims of old, and new visitor attractions appeared including specialist Law and Order museums. At the very end of the 20thC lavish Lottery funding for a variety of major projects promised to take Ripon boldly into the new Millennium.

Mike Younge
Editor

YORKSHIRE MARKET PLACES

Development in this sphere can be summarised in a single word: shrinkage. The medieval market place was huge, often limited not so much by houses as by some major feature such as a castle ditch or a churchyard wall. Knaresborough, Thirsk and Richmond for example all extended to their castle gates, while Bedale, Masham, Northallerton and dozens of other Yorkshire towns had their market places limited in one direction by their parish church. Skipton's market street was exceptional in that it was almost closed off at the northern end by the combination of an adjoining church and castle.

Most markets seem to have come into existence - or at least were first chartered - within two or three hundred years of the Norman conquest. When Domesday Book was compiled in 1086 there were about 50 markets listed in England, and two fairs. Ripon was not included amongst them yet in 1228 the Canons claimed to have had a market and fair since Athelstan's time. At a later date Ripon had both winter and summer fairs, presumably held in the Market Place, but the number of markets increased enormously over the whole of England so that Yorkshire alone had at least 54 in the 16thC, even after excluding the unsuccessful market villages.

The typical market town had far more open spaces than we might now expect. The presence of orchards, garden plots and stock-garths made the distinction between town and countryside much less obvious than it is today, and the town's arable open fields extended the vista. Naturally enough the open spaces were utilised, sometimes for specialised markets which have retained names like Horsefair, but also for separate churches independent of the parish church. They were created within the market squares of Richmond, Malton and many other places, and it may be that churchyards and market areas were almost indistinguishable at one time, for the holding of markets in churchyards had to be banned nationally in 1285. This can hardly have been the case at Pontefact though, where a whole new market suburb known as Westcheap (literally the 'cheap' or market, west of the castle and the ancient borough) was established on a virgin site in 1255 before a new church of St. Giles was built within it.

Whether churches were early encroachers on market spaces, or vice versa, the principal shrinkage of these areas over the centuries has undoubtedly been due to the market activities themselves.

Temporary stalls erected on market day were an unsatisfactory substitute for proper premises, and it seems that butchers, who were in the habit of slaughtering livestock in the market area, were the first to press for permanent quarters. They became known as the Shambles, every town had one, and they were always found adjoining the market square though the name has often disappeared since. The first permanent shops in Knaresborough were the Shambles, and since 17thC records show that many of the shops on the south-west side of the square were still occupied by butchers, it seems likely that that was where they began. Once the principle of a permanent Shambles was established, all the other trades followed suit, and soon the principal street or square was lined with shops where the goods were made as well as being sold.

Markets of course required regulation, and in the early years this was done by 'Pie Powder' courts (from pieds poudreux or 'dusty feet' - a reference to the traders or merchants using the market). Market tolls often formed a sizable proportion of the town's income and were levied on every item sold within its bounds. This meant that the boundary had to be clearly marked - often by a bank and ditch with defined entrances on the main streets - in the absence of town walls. By 1600 almost every market had a tollbooth where market bells were rung, toll charges were displayed and standard measures were kept to check those used by traders. Often it was built over a covered market area and many have survived, though they are not always recognisable. In Tudor times, when many tollbooths or market halls were built, most buildings were timber-framed. Stonework was often added as a later facade or they might be completely rebuilt. A fairly typical progress is found at Knaresborough, where the tollbooth had cellars used for the town gaol while the ground floor was taken over for weavers' shops and the upper floor went through various stages of occupation before becoming the site of the 19thC town hall.

Naturally enough, shops would later be built adjoining the market hall to form an island block in the middle of the square. It would serve to divide the market space into several portions, each devoted to the sale of a different product. In addition, some attempt was made to impose rudimentary hygiene on the area by making the highest point the Cornhill, where the grain was sold, the central area the cloth market, while the lowest point was reserved for the town dung heap where waste vegetable produce was thrown after the market was over.

At Knaresborough the 17thC market regulations required those designated as the 'Gatherers of the Markett Sweepings' to "sufficiently dress(i.e. clean) the market place within the four great chanells, and the Linn (i.e.linen) cloth market, and likewise that place where roots, cabbages and apples are removed to". The last place was the dung heap and is shown on a contemporary map as adjoining the town ditch, which carried waste water (and no doubt all the rubbish) over the cliff upon which Knaresborough was conveniently sited.

Other towns would have had to do the best they could with their waste, but its ultimate destination was always the nearest river - not a hygienic solution bearing in mind that its water was used for a multitude of purposes, though hopefully not for drinking. The market was thus in the long run a likely source of infection as well as profit, yet it brought trade to the town and could not be disposed of. Even when in the 18thC private trading took the wholesale business from the market square into the taverns, individual purchases were still struck in the open and have of course continued up to the present day. Yet it is useful to remember that the areas retained for market day use are mere shadows of their former selves, so small that local people of five centuries and more ago would feel impossibly confined were they to revisit their former haunts.

Dr M. Turner

RIPON MARKET PLACE: THE EARLY YEARS

Its buildings have been many times reconstructed but its boundaries, as shown on plans, disclose a market place laid out in early 13thC fashion on the largest area high enough above the rivers to be well drained ground, sufficiently level that traders' carts would not slide away.

Ripon developed nothing more than informal market trading before 1215 and a market place did not feature in its topography. Before 1215 the archbishopric had been for long periods vacant, inhibiting the formal establishment of a Market. Then Walter De Gray, the Chancellor of King John from 1204, was nominated Archbishop of York. He was an extremely able administrator and his establishment of a formally regulated market place was created by (a) establishing a defined trading area or 'marketsteading', (b) by surrounding that with carefully measured houseplots and (c) recruiting craftsmen to inhabit them on attractive tenancies called *burgage* holdings.

Each burgage was a strip of land (a 'toft') with a dwelling place occupied by a freeman paying a fixed customary rent to the Lord of the Manor. In 1532 Ripon had 202 (and 'a half') burgages, most paying 4 pence a year and sited around a huge rectangle about twice the size of the present Market Place. Their frontages were either 30 feet or 15 feet wide. The original unit of measurement appears to have been the ell (45 inches), so these plots were predominantly 8 ells wide, which appears to have been the standard width of burgage frontages in Northern England. The boundaries along the market's original eastern side indicate an overall length of 160 ells from Kirkgate Head to Allhallowgate, providing space for 20 burgages (all 8 ells, 30 feet wide). Some burgages along the western end of Allhallowgate formed the marketstead's north-eastern corner where the place-name Finkle Street comes from *Finkel*, an Anglo-Scandinavian dialect word for a corner. The location of the original Market Cross, at the centre of the marketstead beside Cross Lane (now Lavender Alley), is exactly at the mid-point of a 160 by 80 ell rectangle.

That 5-acre site provided a clearly defined area within which traders and customers could expect protection against fraud and immediate redress of grievances. Common law definitions for all weights and measures began to be established only in the late 12thC.

Clause 35 of the Great Charter - 'There shall be one measure of wine throughout our whole kingdom.....of ale....grain....dyed cloth....measures' - completed in 1215 their regulation at the time this marketsteading was being established. Walter de Gray had been one of the negotiators when that charter was drawn up.

From about 1216 - 20 the Archbishop drew annually a guaranteed income from the new inhabitants: rent for their burgages, novel types of income such as money-rents, market place and bridge tolls to offset the declining value of older (and fixed) labour services from his manor. That, not the creation of a market, may have been his principal motive because he had set about completing the reconstruction of the Minster. A Market appurtenant to his manor could generate a substantial income for that purpose. As the new building neared completion (1224) he transferred the relic of St Wilfrid to a new shrine at the east end of its presbytery, encouraging visits to it by providing pilgrims with remission of 30 days penance. Their increased offerings funded reconstruction work. Their physical needs increased the marketstead's cash flow. The busiest time for trade was when the saint's relic in its splendid casing was carried in procession around the market. The Minster's fabric funds and the trade of the market both benefited from Walter De Gray's strategies.

The Archbishop's palace was one of several occupied intermittently during their peripatetic lives. They brought a considerable train of clerical lawyers, clerks and the servants who sustained their retinue's communal life. Considerable quantities of high quality foodstuffs would be required for the archbishop's household and noble guests. Their arrival also brought suitors. All brought an appreciable amount of trade to the fledgeling market. Many needed lodging, food and drink, horse shoeing, renewal of worn harness, boots, shoes. They might purchase new goods and stock up with textiles, leather and metal ware before leaving.

The distribution of burgages around this marketstead suggests that less than half of the expected house-places were taken up or built upon during its early years. Those on its western side have a noticeably different lay-out from those on the east, the result of its later completion. Mary Mauchline has shown that from 1230 to 1340 well-established groups of merchants lived here and lists of poll tax payers in 1377 indicate the marketstead was thriving: the tax gatherers listed them as inhabitants of a distinct ward. Between 1215 and 1377 the market had completely changed the configuration of Ripon: 39% of all its tax-payers lived around the Marketstead. They paid 49% of the town's tax; they were the most prosperous of its lay inhabitants.

Occupations stated in the poll tax returns reveal a pattern familiar in late medieval urban economies. The wealthiest were two 'merchants', grocers who maintained stocks of imported goods for retail. Second wealthiest were the food and drink traders; then leather workers (mostly shoemakers); then mercers, drapers and tailors, the clothing trades. Tax returns cannot point out a distinctive feature that could extend a market's reach beyond its immediate locality but a strange 14thC poem listing English places and whatever its composer principally associated with them singled out its horse market: 'Palfrey of Ripon.....Colt of Rievaulx'. Palfreys were saddle-horses; they were the most used by those who in the Middle Ages could afford horses; they were to the medieval economy what family saloons were to the 1920s and 30s. The Horsefair (now North Street) formed the north-western side of the marketstead and existed by 1229.

When vacant plots around the young marketstead had been occupied, competition for trading space led to encroachments on the common soil, creating the pronounced bulge of the frontages on the western side. This was one form of in-filling, an encroachment on the common soil of maturing towns. In the 14th and 15thC another infilling process occurred by which stalls grouped on the open space around the Market Cross became permanent structures with living accommodation, some being given burgage status. Although the present-day 'islands' of shops and houses are later rebuildings, the Flesh Shambles which stood along the middle of what is now Queen Street is the only one of the medieval in-fills to have vanished, demolished piecemeal 1902-5. Gifts of some properties to chantries show that by 1450 the open space was limited to a triangular space called by then the Old Marketstead. Fishgate (Fishergate from the 18thC) and the passages either side of the Flesh Shambles were narrow footways until road widening was undertaken at the end of the 19thC. Crossgate (now Lavender Alley) remains a pedestrian way.

At the centre of the infills The Cross stood on a stone pavement. It was roofed to protect the Corn Market which was held there. At the end of the market day, grain which had fallen out of sample bags and sacks was gathered from the raised pavement for the use of the Wakeman, a perquisite of office called 'The Market Sweepings'. To one side of The Cross was the Lord of the Manor's Tollbooth. Its Hall or Court Room was on the first floor over an open sided space which by 1533 protected five stalls and a workshop 'under *le tolle Bothe*'. Nearby was another manorial structure, the Common Bakehouse.

The southern half of the market place was never in-filled and apparently some of its southern side was partially empty. About 1538 John Leland noted that 'the very place where the *Market stede* and the heart of the town is, was sometime called Holly Hill of (from) the holly trees there growing.' Because the northern half was so built up, market day trading from covered waggons and rented stalls was concentrated on this area which is now 'the' Market Place and the substance of this book is the history of the dwelling houses, shops and banks in this part of the original market place.

Dr W. Petchey

RIPON MARKET PLACE: THE LATER YEARS

In the early 17thC, following the Town Book of 1598, the James Ist Borough Charter of 1604, and the consolidation of the guilds, the governance of Ripon and its trade and industry were set for a century or more.

What was the scene over which the controlling burgesses presided ? The Market Square had settled to its present dimensions, but where exactly was the cross of stone standing in the Tollbooth which in 1612 was 'moved from the place where it stood above 16ft high' ? What of the surrounding buildings ? This was a period of great rebuilding and although much is hidden by later construction, only the Wakeman's House after several facelifts now presents a 17thC or earlier frontage to the street scene.

Celia Fiennes, visiting Ripon in 1697, wrote that the houses were mostly built of stone. There was 'a large market place with a high cross of several steps........We were there the market day when provisions were very plentiful and cheap...........notwithstanding, some of the inns are very dear to strangers that they impose on'. The cross must have been decayed for in 1680 William Gibson had left £50 to the Corporation for building a cross in the market place. Action followed at last in 1702 when with subscriptions from the Archbishop of York, the Chapter, local gentry and principally John Aislabie of Studley (Mayor at the time), the obelisk designed by Nicholas Hawksmoor was erected - the earliest freestanding obelisk in England. Hawksmoor's project for paving the Square was not undertaken and various supporting embellishments were soon removed; interestingly the plinth was to be 9ft above the step 'set rough.....to keep idle persons from making letters and writing what they please upon it, and doing other Mischieves and Brutalities'.

Repairs to the Obelisk were carried out in 1735 and there was major renovation in 1781 after which the present misleading tablet was attached to the south face. A palisade was removed and four smaller columns erected at the corners.

Much re-building was going on during this period; a rain water head (now removed) on the Halifax Bank building, was dated about 1730 and the upper storeys of several other properties are of Georgian date. This culminated in Wyatt's Town Hall of 1800, though some earlier structures must have remained. As Tuting notes 'Now1842 - not one thatched roof'.

The Market Square was a busy place - in addition to the weekly markets several fairs were held for the sale of horses, cattle, sheep and leather, all monitored by the Corporation. In 1660 the Town Clerk was sent to Masham to proclaim the 'Forth Night' Fair, and in 1669 when Boroughbridge petitioned for five new fairs the Archbishop was urged to intervene as this would be detrimental to trade in Ripon. The timing of the fairs was a matter of concern to the Corporation; in 1683 they suggested to the archbishop that the two great horse fairs should be held on Lady Day and Lammas and in 1707 the spring horse fair was advertised in the London Gazette and notices posted around the country. The Holy Thursday Fair was transferred to the first Thursday in June in 1761, with a sheep fair on the following day, and some years later the Soulmass Fair was brought forward to the 2nd of November. In 1838 it was ordered that four public fairs for the sale of wool should be held yearly in the Old Market Place between May and July. These events drew great crowds and provided an opportunity for hospitality and entertainment - provision for 'Ale at the Cross' is frequently recorded and doubtless there was much available elsewhere.

The hub of commercial activity in the town, the Market Square was also important as the focal point where townsfolk and nearby villagers gathered, often for entertainment but also in celebration or protest as feelings were aroused by both local and national issues. In 1569 Norton and Markenfield mustered support there for the Rising of the North, and in 1642 Sir Thomas Mallorie ousted Maulever's parliamentarian occupation. One of the most tumultuous events must have been the Reform Election of 1832 when, after large sums had been spent on free ale and other inducements, the rival supporters converged on the hustings, the 'Blue' Tories via Westgate and the 'Orange' Whigs from Middle Street. The Whig triumph was shortlived in Ripon but reform proceeded apace - the Corporation was re-organised and freedom to trade in the town became free to all. To some Riponians the huge funeral procession of Mrs Lawrence which passed through the town in 1845 must have symbolised the passing of the old order.

Much change followed in the coming years. The development of plate glass changed the appearance of shop fronts, and the coming of the railway must have increased trade for the cabbies. In 1858 the Crimean cannon was 'inaugurated' in an enclosure south of the cross (it was later removed to Kirkgate) and in 1871 a drinking fountain was presented - also to be moved later. The Watchmen who had patrolled the Square were superseded by police in 1874 and their sentry boxes removed. Later the four stone lights which stood at the corners of the Obelisk were replaced by lamps on the sides of the Square, and at the end of the 19thC trees were planted despite some opposition. 'Lavishly appointed toilets with flowers and seats above' were provided in 1899.

There were recurrent complaints about the filth and disturbance caused by the selling of livestock and at last in 1900 the Corporation decided to concrete the Square. Another nuisance was the noise and disturbance of the Martinmas Hiring and other Fairs, particularly as steam-driven roundabouts took over from less sophisticated entertainments. There was also resentment that market stalls were being taken over by traders from elsewhere to the detriment of the local community.

At the beginning of the 1900s all the streets opening onto the Market Place were widened, and in the following decade there was a good deal of re-building and re-fronting in a variety of styles. The Cabmen's Shelter was provided by Miss Carter in 1911. Cattle sales were also eventually removed from the Square. The Thursday Market continued to flourish, though increasingly dominated by traders from outside, and local shopkeepers gave way to national multiples. The Market Place ceased to be a residential area but it remained at the heart of the City; coronations and jubilees were celebrated and with the World Wars and the establishment of the Army Camp, military parades were frequent.

Whit Walks, when hundreds of children carrying banners and flowers gathered in the Square, continued until the 1930s. The invasion of the motor vehicle was inexorable and gradually the Square became a parking ground - spaces were marked out in 1968 and traffic management is still a matter of contention.

Change there will be, but tradition will survive. The Hornblower will set the watch at the corners of the Cross, the Bellman will open the Thursday Market, and St Wilfrid will continue to start his annual progress from the Town Hall.

Ted Pearson

RIPON MARKET PLACE: THE FUTURE

A striking feature of the Market Place seen in the pictures of this book is the wide range of events for which it was used before World War II: fairs, markets, rallies and parades for instance. It was a safe place for people, mainly on foot, but with room for vehicles. Motors cars were at first a welcome novelty on the Square and surrounding streets but then, as their numbers grew and their speeds increased, they threatened to stifle more leisurely acrtivities.

By the 1970s the narrow medieval streets were at times choked with traffic, including many heavy goods vehicles cutting across from the Skipton - Harrogate trans-Pennine route towards the North. Its continued growth threatened pedestrians, polluted the air and damaged property, to an extent that inhibited trade and discouraged any improvement or development. (There was however a benefit: much of the central part of the city escaped the kind of 'inappropriate' redevelopment that spoiled other market towns).

The central square of the Market Place was devoted to car parking; that it was free was a matter of some civic pride ! Its convenience and popularity no doubt helped to bolster Ripon's flagging trade for a decade or two, but people forgot its spaciousness and if they stood a while to gaze at the surrounding buildings they risked being knocked down !

Effective remedies required the diversion of most of this traffic away from the Market Place and at least the narrowest streets. There were various schemes over the years, all expensive, that progressed through the lengthy planning and funding processes to different extents before being abandoned. The difficulties were aggravated by the reorganisation of Local Government in 1974 resulting in the City of Ripon, an independent borough, being subsumed into Harrogate District, which became a constituent of North Yorkshire rather than of the West Riding of Yorkshire as hitherto.

Eventually everyone agreed that the County would have to build a proper by-pass for the north-south A61 to the east and to improve the east-west B6265 across the city. During the early 1990s these works (which were very expensive mainly because 3 complex bridges were needed) were analysed, designed, funded and finally approved.

Construction began with a new east-west route, avoiding the Market Place, and in 1996 the by-pass itself was opened amidst much jubilation. Though there were some teething troubles, there was an immediate improvement in the environment of the city centre, but the Market Place was still dominated by parked cars.

The County's plans for these major traffic changes did not address improvement of the Square itself, which is owned and controlled by Harrogate Borough Council. The latter was beginning the lengthy process of developing a District Local Plan which initially included few changes from the status quo. Ripon Civic Society saw no sign of imaginative thinking in either of the Local Authorities about exploiting the forthcoming reduction of traffic to rejuvenate the

Market Place, which is regarded as an asset second only to the Cathedral, and decided to make a special study of what might be done.

A group of committed and well-qualified members began by considering the Market Place itself, but soon realised that the principal streets, traffic flows and parking would have to be included as well. To cut a long story short: a brief but radical paper was published and widely circulated early in 1995 and generated considerable interest along with some controversy. The most important result was that officers of both the Local Authorities recognised the merit of many of the new proposals and began working together and with the City Council, Civic Society and other bodies to develop them, and later to seek funding from the Heritage Lottery Fund. The County Council carried out several experimental rearrangements of the traffic and eventually what you see today was approved. The refurbishment of the streets to the east of the Market Place and near the Cathedral has already been completed.

Meanwhile, the Borough Council worked on the redesign of the Market Place itself. The final plan is very similar to the Civic Society's proposals: the whole central area will be re-paved in stone; two avenues of mature trees will be planted; the toilets will be moved elsewhere, leaving a clear space between the Town Hall and Obelisk which will remain as the central and dominant feature; some car parking will continue but on only the northern half, and it will not be free; the taxi-rank will be moved across the street; lighting and furniture will be replaced; and all the surrounding streets and footpaths will be distinctively repaved.

These changes will greatly enhance the whole Market Place for the pedestrian, whilst retaining the traffic pattern that is now established. Funding has now been allocated for these considerable changes and work began in the spring of 2001. The newly created open space will give scope not only for use by people who just want to walk about in comfort or sit and chat to friends during their shopping trips, but also for better staging and management of the many open air events that are an important constituent of Ripon's festivals and civic occasions. The road in front of the Town Hall can be closed when required without serious disruption of traffic. The popular weekly Thursday and Saturday markets will continue, the former occupying the entire area but with re-aligned stalls to make it more convenient for shoppers and traders. Thus the Market Place will be restored in the 21stC to the literally central role in the commercial, cultural and social life of the city that it has fulfilled for 800 years.

Brian Carroll

RIPON MARKET PLACE: AROUND THE SQUARE

1 Market Place (East)

This burgage at the corner of the Market Place and Kirkgate was once much larger than at present because of 20thC widening at Kirkgatehead. In 1672 it is shown as being taxed for 6 hearths and being occupied by Thomas Hebden who was a grocer. His ownership is confirmed by the 1675 Burgage Survey where it is said to have consisted of one toft, one croft and five shops and to have been inherited by Thomas from his father George. However, it would appear that soon after this, Thomas must have sold or possibly mortgaged the southern part of the property because in 1686 one Thomas Thompson sold this part of the property for £100 to John Sedgwick, mercer. Sedgwick, who was to be Mayor of Ripon in 1701-2 and 1715-16, was the nephew of Thomas Hebden.

Thomas Hebden died in 1691 and after the death of his widow the northern part of the property where he himself had been living also went to Sedgwick, so the property was again united. John Sedgwick died in 1720 and the property was left to his widow for life, and afterwards to his four daughters. His son received only a bottle of wine which sounds rather like parental disapproval although it may have been merely that the son had received his share of the family property earlier.

The Average Award of 1747 confirms that the property was held by Sedgwick's heirs although the widow and one of the daughters had died. In 1764 the three surviving daughters and the husbands of two of them sold the property for £400 to Christopher Braithwaite, mercer. The deed refers to four shops, two gardens or orchards and two stables, and the property is said to be occupied by four tenants, one of whom, Sarah Haddon, owned the Unicorn Inn next door. The date 1765 found on the gable end of the property when it was being demolished in 1931 probably records the rebuilding in brick by Braithwaite, the new owner.

Soon after this Christopher Braithwaite changed his name to Oxley as a result of an inheritance, and then in 1776 sold this property for £750 to John Raggett of Markenfield Hall.

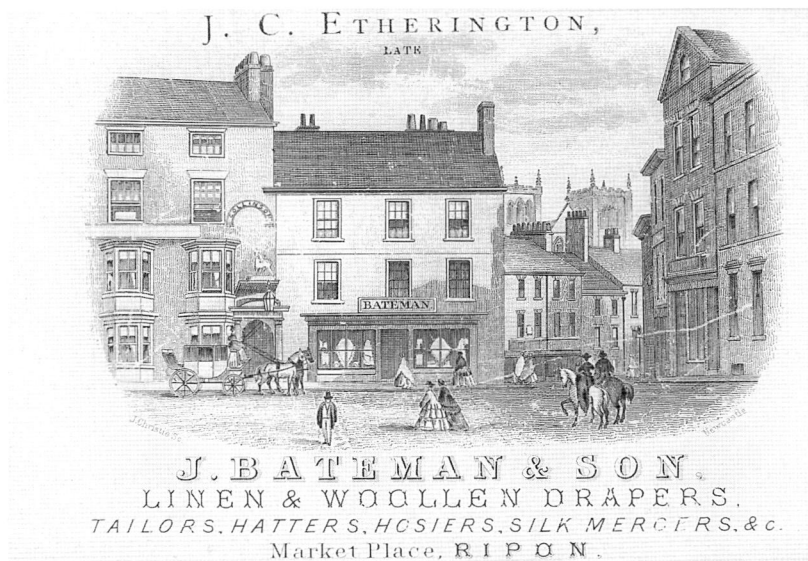

J. C. ETHERINGTON,
LATE

J. BATEMAN & SON,
LINEN & WOOLLEN DRAPERS,
TAILORS, HATTERS, HOSIERS, SILK MERCERS, &c.
Market Place, RIPON.

Probably because of the rebuilding, the premises then consisted of two houses again occupied by tenants. The Humphries Survey of 1800 showed the property owned by Widow Raggett. It then passed to their son, another John, and was left in his will in 1808 to his widow and his brother for life, after which it was to go to his two nephews. However, only one of these nephews survived to enjoy the property and so it came into the possession of the other, Thomas Raggett, a London merchant, who in 1816 sold it to Elizabeth Sophia Lawrence of Studley Royal. (The price paid, £1890, included another Raggett property).

The two houses on this site are said to have been rented at this time by Samuel Coates the Younger (*) and James Morley, surgeon. The property was to remain part of the Studley estate for the rest of the century for most of which it was to be occupied by members of the Bateman family who were tailors and drapers. The first member of the family to feature was Joseph who was admitted as a freeman in 1821. Some time near the end of the century the Batemans were replaced as tenants by James C. Etherington, also a draper.

In 1903 the Marquess of Ripon, the owner of the Studley estate, sold the property to Sir Christopher Furness, later Lord Furness of Grantley Hall, who had made his money out of shipping. After the death of Lord Furness his son began to reduce his connection with the area and sold the property in 1919 to the partners of Becket and Co, the Leeds-based private bank. In the following year this bank was amalgamated with what was later known as the Westminster Bank. The Bank did not themselves occupy the property at this time.

A trade directory of 1922 shows that the Etheringtons had been followed in the property by Dixon Stephenson who described himself as a "robe specialist", but a 1927 directory omits No.1 Market Place altogether. However NatWest Group archives reveal that the property was let for £120 per annum from 1924 to 1930 to a Captain and Mrs. Hartley, so it seems that they must have been

running the Blue Bird cafe which was demolished in 1931 as a result of the Ripon Corporation scheme for widening Kirkgatehead. The corner property was subsequently rebuilt further back in the typical bank style of the period and in 1932 the Westminster Bank moved there from the premises it formerly occupied in Fishergate.

The Bank occupied the premises until after its amalgamation in 1971 with the National Provincial Bank; the newly amalgamated bank, the National Westminster, decided to give up No.1 and concentrate on its site on the south side of the Market Place. Since the 1970s the property has been occupied by the Skipton Building Society.

Jean Denton & Wendy Hunter.

(* In 1771 a Samuel Coates had founded the local bank which later became known as Coates, Pearson and Coates with its headquarters in Knaresborough and a branch in Ripon, and in 1784 Samuel Coates Jr. was listed in Bailey's Directory as a linen draper in Ripon, so it is quite possible that the Batemans who began to occupy the property in the early 19thC took over premises already in use as a draper's shop).

1   *The Market Place depicted by Julius Caesar Ibbetson in the period 1805-17. The mini-obelisks were removed in 1882.*

2-3 Market Place (East)

The name of the Unicorn hotel may well go back to the late Middle Ages when inns were required to carry a distinctive sign which could be recognised by the illiterate. Many signs were inspired by the Church's Bestiary - a popular publication which described and illustrated the many wild creatures referred to in the Bible, mostly quite fanciful in their detail. Amongst them was the milk-white Unicorn, part-horse, part-lion, even part antelope, famed for its strength and fierceness, and best known for the twisted horn set in its forehead.

The Church's dominating presence in medieval Ripon would readily explain why a town inn should choose its name from the religious symbolism of the period, particularly in view of the common belief that a Unicorn drinking cup was proof against all poisons ! It is also likely that the Unicorn Inn would accommodate pilgrims to the Shrine of St. Wilfrid - the tourists of the day - as well as many of those who came to Ripon on church business. It may in fact have begun as a Guest House of the Archbishop of York whose palace lay close by.

The Poll Tax returns of 1379 give no inn names, but 3 'brewsters' are listed around the Market Place, and it is tempting to see one of them, Thomas de Ledes, who paid the high rate of 24d, as innholder of the Unicorn.

The earliest specific reference to the Unicorn so far found dates to 1626 which raises the alternative possibility that its name was inspired by the Unicorn added

to the Royal Coat of Arms by James I, who granted Ripon two charters and also happened to stay in the town in 1617. The 1626 reference concerns another important visitor, Edward Alleyn, a theatre actor-manager from London who became Keeper of the King's Beasts and then went on to found Dulwich College (1619). In July 1626 he signed legal papers in 'the house of Margaret Turner at the sign of the Unicorn in Ripon' whilst on a journey north - and then died in November of the same year.

This invaluable reference links the Unicorn to the 'house of Edward Turner in the Market Place' where the Corporation held its meetings in 1611 whilst a new town house was being built. There were many later occasions when the Corporation favoured the Unicorn but this is almost certainly the earliest surviving example. After his first wife died in 1603, Edward married a widow Margaret Allanson the same year, and she ran the Unicorn after his death in 1624. By the time of Alleyn's visit in 1626, twice widowed Margaret had also survived plague in the town in 1625. She lived until 1646 and the following year Charles I spent two nights in Ripon under armed guard, but it is unlikely that he was lodged at the Unicorn. Following Margaret Turner's death the inn passed to Thomas Allanson, a son by her first marriage, but the property was very soon sold on to Richard Porter, presumably a family friend since his wife Frances had been bequeathed Margaret's 'best gown and my best petticoat'.

The Hearth Tax returns of 1672 show the Unicorn possessing 8 hearths, such as a large establishment would require, and Richard Porter figures in the 1675 Survey of Burgages. The following year however he died and the Unicorn passed to his son, Richard Porter junior, but within 3 years both he and his wife were dead. At that stage Ellen Horner, one of Richard's sisters, inherited the hostelry, but when she died in 1693 it passed to her three married sisters, a decision that fragmented the ownership of the Unicorn for 50 years.

In 1697 Ripon was visited by the much travelled Celia Fiennes who recorded in her diary that in Ripon 'some of the inns are very dear to strangers that they can impose on' - hopefully the Unicorn was not one of these! During the reign of Queen Anne, Francis Cowling emerges as the Unicorn innkeeper, clearly bent on becoming the full owner too, and between 1704 and 1707 he succeeded in purchasing two of the three shares from the relatives of Ellen Horner. A busy man, he is later (1715) found being paid 8s. 4d for five quarts of wine 'at the Cross' at the proclamation of the accession of George I, and collecting money 'for a Plate to be run for upon Ripon Common' (1717).

When he eventually retired to Richmond (by 1729), he mortgaged his 2/3 holding to his nephew Cuthbert Cowling for £220. His nephew went on to inherit the property 'known by the name or sign of the Unicorn' on Francis's death in 1734, and ten years later he was able to secure the missing 1/3 share, so returning the inn once more to a single ownership (1744).

The very next year however Cowling sold the Unicorn for £410 to the existing tenant landlord, William Haddon, and his wife Sarah. This was a significant event as the Haddon family was to control the affairs of the Unicorn for the rest of the 18thC.

Nearly all the timber buildings around the Square were rebuilt in brick during the 18thC, and the evidence suggests that in the case of the Unicorn the rebuilding was the work of William Haddon between 1745 and his death in 1748. Over the next twenty years his widow Sarah extended the Unicorn premises at the rear, and then in 1769 was involved in a major property deal with her neighbour on the north side, Henry Kirkby, and a third party John Ullithorne. In a complex agreement Ullithorne appears to have bought Kirkby's property (for £410) and then immediately divided it, selling the half abutting the Unicorn to Sarah Haddon (for £210). There is reference to the central passageway which can still be seen. It seems that this half continued as a separate unit (the later No. 3 Market Place), and in the mid-19thC was a grocer's shop (as described later).

It was in the time of Sarah Haddon that the Unicorn achieved widespread if not national fame through the exploits of Tom Crudd, who as 'Boots' had the task of helping travellers remove their outdoor footware and put on slippers. Crudd had a natural 'Mr Punch' face and his party trick was to ask for a coin which he then held between nose and chin, to the great merriment of the visitors. But Crudd kept the coin and so had the last laugh!

Sarah Haddon died in 1774 and the Unicorn passed to her son John and his wife Alice. He himself however died only six years later (1780) making the inn once again the responsibility of a widow. At some point in the 1780s John Fairgray appears on the scene as innkeeper, a position which he held for some twenty years, but the ownership remained with Alice Haddon from 1780 to 1812.

Ripon Corporation followed earlier precedent by meeting at the Unicorn whilst the new Town Hall was under construction (1799), and Fairgray was paid for the use of his rooms. Already a councillor, he went on to become Mayor of Ripon in 1806/7, the first Unicorn proprietor known to have achieved this honour. He died young in 1809 and his portrait hangs in the Mayor's Parlour.

In the early 19thC the Unicorn bustled with activity, servicing long-distance stage coaches and private carriages, and used for a variety of events and meetings including the local Coroner's Court. A schedule of 1817 contains reference to a Breakfast Room, Coffee Room, Travellers Room, Bow and Back Parlours, Bar and Tap Room, kitchen and pantry, ale and wine cellars, stables and lofts, and a coach office.

In 1805 the Ripon Loyal Volunteer Corps entertained their colonel there, the dinner ending 'with the utmost conviviality and mirth', but only a few years later Ripon innkeepers were complaining bitterly at having a regiment of regular infantry billeted upon them.

In 1812 ownership of the inn passed on Alice Haddon's death to her nephew John Haddon Askwith, then of Sleningford Hall; a surviving insurance policy of June 1814 shows the new owner insuring the Unicorn and its contents for £3000. In June 1817 Askwith leased 'that well-known capital and accustomed Inn and Posting House called the Unicorn Inn' to Mr Haseldine Sharpin of York for 7 years, but within four years (1821) Askwith

WONDERFUL MAGAZINE.

This Extraordinary Man lived long at an Inn at Rippon in Yorkshire. By nature & habit he acquired the power of holding a piece of Money between his Nose & Chin.

His chief employment was waiting on the Customers &c. From the circumstance of his Cleaning their Shoes & Boots he went by the Name of Old Boots.

Drawn from the Life by Tim' Bobin.   J. Strange Sculp.

OLD BOOTS of RIPPON in YORKSHIRE.
Published by C. Johnson March 1st 1793.

RIPON, YORKSHIRE.

18

had sold it to Elizabeth Sophia Lawrence of Studley Royal (for £4500).

In the 1830s the Unicorn was caught up in the frenzy of local politics that followed the passing of the Great Reform Bill in 1832, serving as the base for the Tory Party during local elections. Victory at the polls justified 'splendid dinners' such as that provided by 'Mr. Thwaites, the spirited landlord of the Unicorn' in 1835. Richard Thwaites was still proprietor in 1842 when he resigned after several years work as a City Councillor. During that time the wedding of Victoria and Albert was duly celebrated (Feb.1840) by a Ball in the Town Hall preceded by a dinner in the Unicorn.

The Studley Royal estate was to retain ownership of the hotel for many years, but Unicorn proprietors came and went. In 1848 when the railway had just arrived, John and Ann Cleminshaw were in charge. By 1851, when full census details first become available, Ann (aged 67), presumably now a widow, had become 'Head of Family'. The resident staff included a cook, waiter, kitchen maid, two housemaids and still a 'Boots' - then 27 year old William Maude who

later was to die 'thrown from the bus he was driving and run over, at Studley' (July 1859). The previous year Charles Dodgson had been a guest of the Unicorn.

From the early 1860s until his death in 1889 Robert Ellington Collinson was the highly regarded landlord who also managed to find time to be Mayor of Ripon for four consecutive terms (1876-80). After their wedding in 1863 the Prince and Princess of Wales visited Ripon, staying overnight at Studley Royal. Thereafter Collinson claimed royal patronage for the Unicorn - did the couple pop in for a quick one ?

A decade later (by 1875) Collinson acquired the tenancy of the shop next door (No.3), which the Unicorn had lost control of since the days of Sarah Haddon, and incorporated it into his hotel, giving the Unicorn the extended facade which it has had ever since. By then he had remarried after the death of

19

his first wife in 1870, and he and his second wife Eliza were to have four children to add to the three from the first marriage. The 1881 census records not only this large family (with two nurses) but also a fully staffed and obviously successful hotel. Collinson, who was also a magistrate and prominent Freemason, died at the Unicorn on Boxing Day 1889, aged 55, and was buried in Holy Trinity churchyard after a full civic funeral.

Following Collinson's death, Bernard and Elizabeth Evans took over the Unicorn and ran it in the 1890s. In 1901 a survey of licensed houses in Ripon revealed that the Unicorn had 24 bedrooms and stabling for over 50 horses, and was deemed the largest family and commercial hotel in the city. However the telephone (No.4) and the motor car had now arrived, and the hotel's motorised omnibus soon replaced the horse-drawn coach which over the years had taken passengers to and from the railway station.

In 1902 the Unicorn was acquired for development by a consortium headed by Sir Christopher Furness of Grantley Hall but attention then shifted to building the Spa Hotel instead, and in 1919 Viscount Furness sold the Unicorn for £8000 to the local Hepworth's Brewery. In 1963 Hepworth's property passed to Vaux Brewery of Sunderland, after which the Unicorn changed hands several times before being acquired by the present owners, David and Maureen Small, in 1983.

Mike Younge

2. *A quiet Square c.1828. Fishergate had not yet been widened.*

3. *The south-east corner of the Square c.1828. The Town Hall was then a recent arrival on the scene (1800).*

4 Market Place (East)

The earliest surviving information relating to the burgage property that now houses Harrison's business, next door to the Unicorn Hotel, comes from the early 17thC when it belonged to the Uckerby family. Soon however it passed into the ownership of the celebrated Hugh Ripley, last Wakeman and three times Mayor, who died in 1637.

The next owners were the Kirkby family, first Alderman Henry Kirkby, Mayor in 1650-1, and then from 1659 his son Edward, also an Alderman and Mayor in 1674/5. A grocer, his house is recorded as having seven hearths in the tax returns of 1672 and is listed in the Burgage Survey of 1675.

After Edward Kirkby died in 1680 the house passed to his son, another Edward, and later to Henry Kirkby (d.1773) who was Mayor both in 1749-50 and in 1764-5. By then the house had been rebuilt in brick with a central passageway, but in 1769, a few years before his death, Kirkby sold the property to John Ullithorne - who immediately sold on the southern half to Sarah Haddon of the Unicorn for £210, leaving the building in divided use from that time to the present day.

It is not clear how Sarah Haddon disposed of her half but by the 1820s, if not earlier, it had become a separate shop (see below) run as a grocer's by Christopher Nelson before 1843, and similarly by John Tuting in the 1850s, '60s, and early '70s.

The northern half, the future No. 4, passed on John Ullithorne's death in 1776 to his widow Sabrina, and then on her death in 1800 to her two married daughters, Rebecca Tripass and Isabella Thompson. In 1807, with Rebecca remarried and Isabella dead, the property was sold on to Robert Williamson (d.1829) and ownership remained with his family until 1841.

Meanwhile, evidence from trade directories indicates that by 1813 No. 4 had become the shop of the bookseller, stationer and active publisher Thomas Langdale. After his death in 1832 his widow Elizabeth ran the business, but in 1836 John Linney, a Quaker printer, took over the tenancy there. In 1840 the business passed to William Harrison, a 23 year old former apprentice, who went on to become a Councillor and also local manager

of the Ripon and Richmond Chronicle (est. 1856). He was a keen antiquary and published the works of his friend, the local historian J. R. Walbran.

However, in 1857, in an odd development, the premises at No.4 appear to have been shared by Harrisons and a Mrs Ann Johnson, who traded there as Johnson & Co and in 1859 even described her company as 'successors to W. Harrison'. Johnson's business was still there in 1875, but had gone by the end of the century.

In 1841 the property was sold by the Williamsons to Christopher Nelson, widower, whose deceased wife had been Robert Williamson's eldest daughter Phillis. Christopher Nelson was a grocer occupying No. 3 (see above) and had been Mayor in 1832-3. It seems that he may already have acquired ownership of No. 3 since on his death in 1843 aged 66, both Nos. 3 & 4 were inherited by his young nephew Nelson Williamson and neice Mary Ann Williamson. Mary Ann went on to marry a certain Victor Dobrovolski, 'from the Empire of Russia', and in 1865, anxious to leave England, she agreed to the sale of their property to the Earl de Grey of Studley Royal. By 1875 the former shop at No.3 had been leased as an extension to the Unicorn Hotel.

Two years later William Harrison died (1867) aged 50, to be succeeded by his 21-year old son, William Harrison junior, who had similar tastes and was a prime mover behind the great Millenary Festival of 1886, after which he published the Millenary History of Ripon (1892) - still a reference work of great value to historians today.

William Harrison junior married Annabella Wells and their son was given the name of William Wells Harrison. In 1914 the firm became William Harrison & Son when William Wells Harrison was taken into the business. Later that year the father died, but so too did the son soon after, in the last year of the Great War. By 1903 the the ownership of No. 4 had passed from the Marquess of Ripon to Viscount Furness, and in 1919 it was offered for sale along with adjacent properties.

Mrs. Harrison, now a widow, carried on the business with difficulty, and in 1920 it was acquired by a former apprentice, Charles Harker. Harker, a city councillor for 22 years, continued the tradition of proprietors of No.4 by becoming Mayor (1925-6, 26-7), and in 1936 organised the centenary celebrations of Harrison's printing and publishing business. A founder member of Ripon's Rotary Club, Harker also printed the local Wakeman magazine. The Freedom of the City was conferred on him in 1958 and he died in 1965 aged 90. At some stage Charles Harker acquired ownership of the property as well as the business, which after his death passed to his daughter Mrs Louie Allan, and thereafter to his grandchildren Peter and John Allan and Mrs Janet Wharton. In 1990 it was acquired wholly by Ted and Janet Wharton.

Mike Younge

4. *The south side of the Square in 1837.*

5 Market Place (East)

Today Morrison's Supermarket stands at No.5 Market Place. In the 18thC the property was 'known by the sign of the White Hart' and was situated on the east side of the Market Place. Christopher Hunton (junior) was the owner in 1731 and lived in the burgage house at the back of the White Hart Inn which was tenanted by Richard Dickenson the innholder.

Christopher Hunton (senior) acquired the property in 1673. William Busfeild had been the previous owner. His widow, Anne, was living in the burgage house when she paid Hearth Tax for eight chimneys in 1672. She died the same year. Prior to William Busfeild the premises had belonged to Phillip White and before that to John Bowes.

The Hunton family lived in and owned the premises for over 100 years. Christopher Hunton (senior) when Mayor in 1686/7 gave in to pride and displayed the town's regalia at his inn, consequently much of it was stolen including badges from the Wakemans belt and horn for which he had to pay a fine of 20 shillings.

In 1737 Christopher Hunton (junior), a saddler by trade, bequeathed all the Market Place property to his son John along with 'my great silver cupp and cover and one great brass candlestick......may allways goe along with the Burrow house.' On John's death in 1774 the property passed to his nephew Matthias Whitehead. The following year William Park, a merchant of Pateley Bridge, purchased the property from Matthias for £460. Two years later in May 1777 William Park and his wife Mary sold it to William Barker the younger, an innkeeper of Ripon, for £580. The indenture describes the burgage house as with 'the late new erected building stables and outbuildings and the ground whereon the same are built also the yard garden and orchard on the backside.' This suggests substantial building work had taken place. To raise the capital of £500 Mr. Barker mortgaged the property for 2000 years to Launcelot Rainforth, a yeoman from Dishforth.

Between 1777 and 1800 the premises were leased, mortgaged or sold in part to several different owners, and entangled with financial provision made for various family members until John Groves sold the property in 1800 to

THE CROWN
Family and Commercial Hotel,
MARKET-PLACE, RIPON.

PRIVATE, PICNIC & OTHER PARTIES,
VISITING

RIPON, STUDLEY, FOUNTAINS ABBEY, HACKFALL, &C.,
CAN BE ACCOMMODATED WITH

Luncheons, Dinners, Conveyances, &c.,
ON THE SHORTEST NOTICE.

EDWARD BLACKER, *Proprietor,*
IMPORTER OF
WINES AND SPIRITS
OF THE CHOICEST QUALITY.

BILLIARDS. - POSTING HOUSE.

Horner Reynard who as a result became the sole owner. More building work had been carried out and described as 'the lately erected long room'. At this time the inn's name was changed to the ' New Inn'. Horner Reynard sold the property in 1805 to William Britain in trust for James Britain for £1164. By 1811 the inn had been renamed again and was now the 'Crown and Anchor', which may mark the acquisition of the premises by Miss Elizabeth Lawrence of Studley Royal.

Throughout the 1820s and until the mid-1830s the Bulmer family kept the Crown and Anchor Inn and Mr. Thomas Blackburn ran a land carriage from here. By 1837 the Blacker family had taken over as innholders and Robert Blacker, his wife Mary, six children, a cook, two servants and an agricultural labourer all lived at the inn.

In Mr. Thirlway's diary on 15th February 1838 he writes about attending a performance of 'The Practical Illusions' in the Long Room at the Crown and Anchor. On another occasion in 1838 he saw a Mr. Irvine ascend 'from the ground to the top window of Mr. Blacker's house, the Crown and Anchor, upon a tightrope amidst a display of fireworks.' Robert Blacker's son Edward continued as innkeeper and then his sister Hannah took over about 1887 when Ann Hewitson became the hotel keeper at the Crown Hotel. The inn was known as the Crown and Anchor during the first part of the 19thC but by the 1850s it was referred to just as 'the Crown' and by the end of the century it was the 'Crown Hotel'. The wooden Crown Inn sign has survived and may be restored to the building. At the end of the century the property through inheritance belonged to the Marquess of Ripon of Studley Royal.

In 1901 an Inquiry was carried out into all the licensed houses in Ripon. The detailed findings record the 'Crown and Anchor' as a free house with 12 bedrooms for visitors.....can dine about 150 at one time.....stabling for 20 horses...... coach house and yard for vehicles.... ' The bedrooms were in 'fair condition' but the sanitary arrangements were 'not good' and 'pigs are kept and allowed to run on the manure pit'.

The Crown Hotel became the possession of Sir Christopher Furness in 1903. A plan to demolish the Unicorn and then to incorporate the upper floors of the Crown Hotel into a large new hotel and build shops on its ground floor was never carried out. The Crown Hotel's licence was not renewed in 1907 and it closed. Croft and Blackburn's motor works took over a 14 year lease in April 1908. They displayed in their showroom in 1914 a 38hp Wolseley motor ambulance presented by Lord Furness to the army.

No.5 was sold by Viscount Furness in 1919 to Messrs George and John Blackburn. The property comprised of business premises and dwelling apartments. Mr. Jonas Gaunt of Appleton's, the pork butcher, after buying No.6 on 18 August 1936 sold most of his backyard to Croft and Blackburn the next day. The business premises were

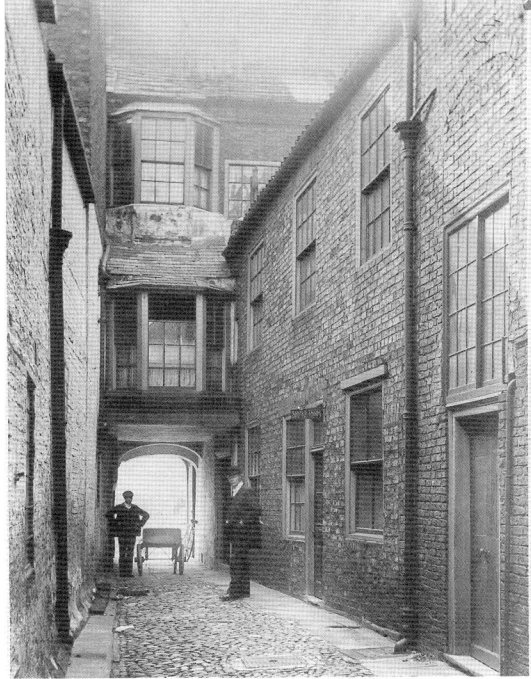

adapted by the motor works for use as a showroom, garage, offices, paint shops, stores, etc. The main changes were to the ground floor. The front of the building became the showroom with the petrol pumps outside.

In 1974 William Morrison Supermarkets plc bought the property. After an appeal in January 1976 permission was given by the Dept of the Environment and construction began on the site in July 1976. The upper rooms facing onto the Market Place were retained for staff and office use. The rest of the motor works buildings were demolished and the site built over. The architects were Messrs. Fletcher Ross and Hickling of Leeds. The new supermarket opened in January 1977.

Anna Horsey

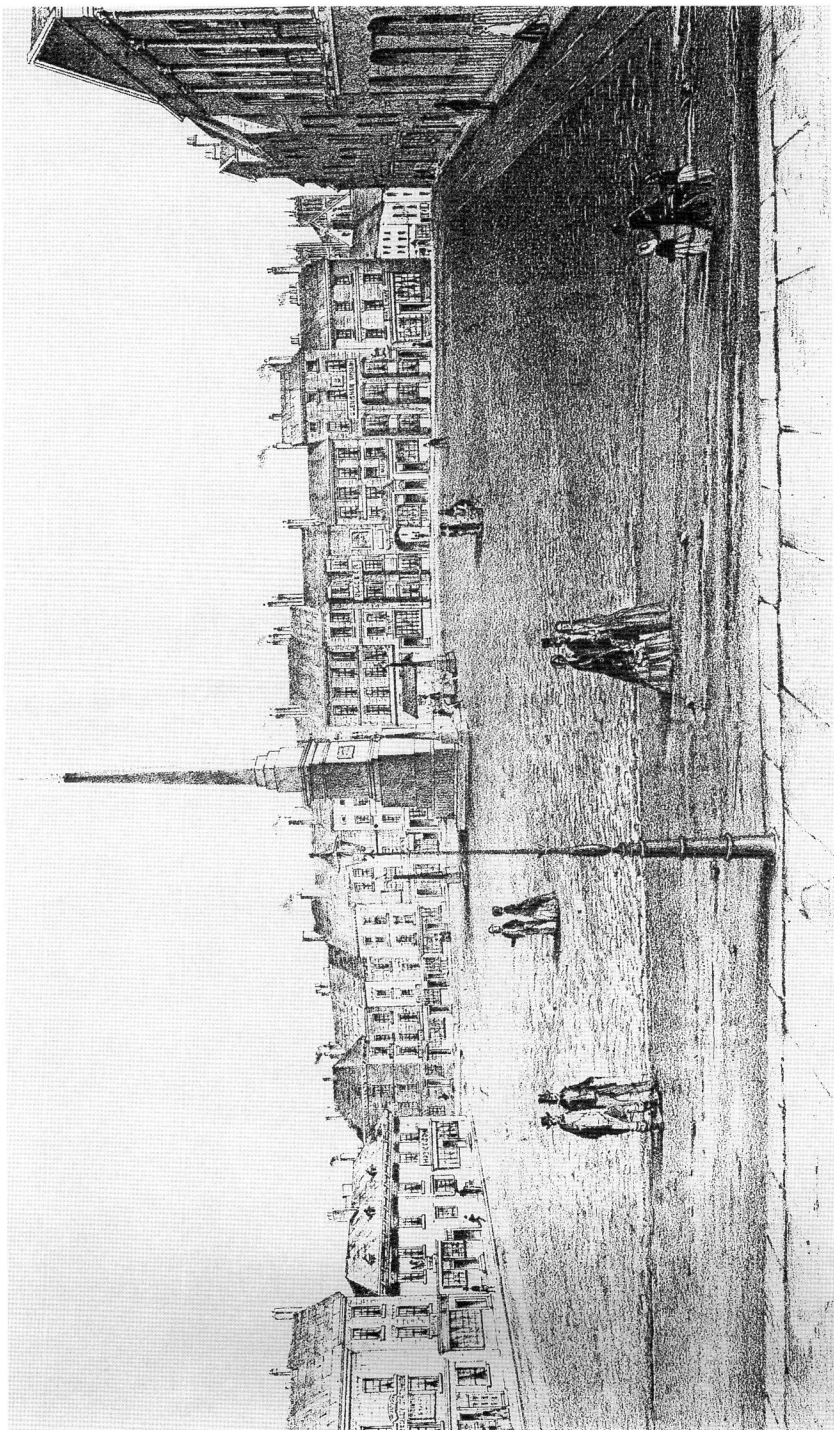

5. *A wide-angle view of the Square c.1850, showing the Watchman's shelter near the obelisk. Gas lighting had now arrived.*

6 Market Place (East)

The Pork Butchers shop known as Appletons at No. 6 Market Place has a long and interesting history. In October 1619 a mercer called George Pulleine died, leaving his property in the Market Place to his elder daughter Alice, born in 1604. George Pulleine who had been Wakeman in 1600 and Mayor in 1608/9 had married William Battie's daughter Alice in 1600. They had a son and two daughters, Alice who married William Underwood esquire, and Anne who inherited other property in the Market Place and married a Mr. Chaytor.

It is George Underwood, son of Alice and William, who claimed the above burgage in the 1675 Inquisition of Burgages, his wife's inheritance. The claim is supported by Robert Atkinson who stated that he had seen the last will and testament or an authentic copy thereof made by George Pulleine in the ecclesiastical court at York where it was proved. Robert Atkinson was described as in possession of the burgage but in what capacity it is not clear. He had married Mary Roades on 27 September 1653 and they had 8 children but only two survived infancy, Elizabeth baptised in 1664 and Jane baptised in 1667. The 1672 Hearth Tax returns show Robert Atkinson responsible for the tax on 4 hearths while next door Mrs. Chaytor had 6. This could well be Anne, younger daughter of George Pulleine. Next door to her is Alderman Chambers and two or three doors further along is John Struther - both these names will appear later in this report.

There is a gap of 30 years before more information is available. During this period the property came into the joint ownership of John Aislabie of Studley Royal and Thomas Emson, gentleman of York. The Register of Deeds in

Wakefield starts in 1704, so these two gentlemen must have been the owners until they sold it in Nov 1709 to Charles Oxley for the sum of £230.

An apothecary and surgeon, Charles Oxley was son of the Charles Oxley who was Master of the Grammar School from about 1668 to 1675. Two weeks before the sale in 1709, Charles Oxley bought a property and two shops adjoining for the sum of £90 from Henry Markingfield, a barber from Bedale, his wife Margaret and son Henry. The property was in the possession of Thomas Cant, the two shops in the possession of James Robinson, all situated in the Old Market Place. On Nov 24 Charles sold this property, but not I think the two shops, to Thomas Emson of York for £60. On the same day he bought the Market Place site from John Aislabie and Thomas Emson as stated above.

The site is described as being between that of Mr. Ridsdale on the north and Mr. Christopher Hunton on the south, and in the possession of George Palliser, 'innholder and foreigner', taken on as an apprentice mercer by John Strother when he was Mayor in 1697/8. As he is classed as a 'foreigner', in other words not from Ripon, he could be a son of the George Palliser from Bishop Thornton whose children Mary and Matthew were baptised in 1674 and 1676.

Mr. Charles Oxley, Mayor in 1720 and 1731, lived in Skellgarth, and his son Charles, also an apothecary and surgeon, and Mayor in 1738, owned the Market Place property between his father's death in 1736 and his own in 1757. According to this will of 1755 he resided in his house in the Market Place and owned 'the next two adjoining', occupied by his sister Mrs. Judith Braithwaite and Mrs. Chambers. As he died without issue, the property passed to his younger brother's son, Charles Oxley. He also died without issue in 1775 so the estate now passed to Christopher Braithwaite, son of Christopher Braithwaite and his wife Judith (nee Oxley), sister to the Charles Oxley who died in 1757.

Christopher Braithwaite, mercer and woollen draper, changed his name to Oxley on inheriting the estate. He was Mayor in 1752, 1766 and 1775. His first wife, Juliana Grainge, gave him two daughters, Frances and Juliana, before she died in 1769. In 1770 he married his cousin Elizabeth Braithwaite, daughter of his uncle Edmund, who bore him two children who died in infancy before she herself died in 1773. His third wife Dorothy Beckwith, daughter of William Beckwith of Lamb Hill, gave him a son Charles Oxley who inherited the estate on his father's death in 1803 and retained it until he died in 1873. His son, Charles Christopher Oxley, sold No.6 Market Place to his tenant Richard Robinson Snow in 1877.

We now start the period of fully documented evidence of occupation up to the present day.

Baines Directory of 1822 lists Carter & Son, jeweller and watchmaker, trading at the address. Willey Edward Carter, son of Rev. John Carter Vicar of Aldborough, paid a fine in 1800 for admission as a Freeman to enable him to trade in Ripon. Born in 1760 he had married Frances James, niece of Mrs. Hardman of York, at St Botolph, Aldersgate St, London in 1785. They had a son, Henry, born in 1795 in Ripon. Willey Carter was Mayor in 1817 and 1829, living in Skellgarth in 1833 before he retired about 1837. He died of old age (82) in London, being buried at Camberwell church in 1842.

Slater's Directory of 1848 shows Henry Carter trading there while the 1851 census shows that he lived there with his wife Ann, four years younger than himself and born at Norton Le Clay, and his daughter Frances, aged 18 and unmarried. On December 6 1856 Henry Carter advertised in the Ripon and Richmond Chronicle that he was having a sale at his shop prior to clearing out the whole stock by 1 May 1857. His retirement plans must have come slightly unstuck as it was not until 21 November 1857 that he was able to place a further notice in the Chronicle to say that on November 23 1857 he was handing over the shop and stock to Richard Robinson Snow.

The 1861 census shows that a considerable number of people were living at what was later to be known as No. 6 Market Place. Firstly there was Richard Robinson Snow, watchmaker and jeweller, aged 42, born at Harewood, with his wife Sarah, 34, from Kirby Overblow, and 7 children. The first 5 children - Elizabeth (13), William Stables (11), Charles Moses (10), Francis (8) and John Henry (5) had all been born at Harewood; Sarah Jane (3) and Emoth (5 months) had been born in Ripon. Then there were two apprentices, James Brooke from Kirby Overblow and John Richardson from Easingwold, together with two servants, Mary West (60) unmarried from Harewood and Elizabeth Scott (23) a widow from Laverton. There was also a visitor, Elizabeth Stubbs (23) from Kirby Overblow.

Ten years later the 1871 census shows that Richard Snow had prospered as he now employed two men and two boys. Family circumstances had changed somewhat. He had a new wife called Mary, born in Bedale and the same age as his previous wife. Son William was working for him as a qualified watchmaker and jeweller, Francis and Sarah were still at school, Charles and Elizabeth had left home, of Emoth there was no mention. Also living there were Henry Soppett (20), an unmarried apprentice from Northallerton and Dinah Ibbotson (24) an unmarried servant from Copt Hewick.

On 2 February 1877 Richard Snow purchased the property from Charles Christopher Oxley, as mentioned earlier. Samuel Wise, solicitor, was also a party. By 1881 Mr. Snow had taken his unmarried son William (31) into partnership as Snow & Son, and he retired to live at 16 Coltsgate Hill in 1893.

Mills and Son,

CERTIFIED OPTICIANS,

By Written Examination.

MILLS & SON
JEWELLERS
SILVERSMITHS
WATCHMAKERS
CERTIFICATED
OPTICIANS
6, Market Place
RIPON

H.M. Silver Charms.
2s. 6d.

H.M. Silver Charms.
2s. 6d.

Mills & Son, Watchmakers & Goldsmiths, Ripon.

From the 1881 census it can be seen that his daughter Elizabeth (32) was now Principal of the Girls' Boarding School at 10 Park Street and his younger daughter Sarah (22) was a teacher there. An aunt of the two girls, Mrs. Aslin, born in Harewood, was also here in some capacity with her children, one of whom, Miss Amy Aslin was Principal of the Girls Boarding School at 10 Park Street in the Directories of 1922, 1927 and 1936.

William Stables Snow had been born in 1850 and continued in the family business with his wife Florence. An agreement was signed in 1894 with the Bradford Old Bank, next door at No.7, concerning walls and drains. William Snow died in 1904 and in 1905 Frederick Mills was in business at No. 6 as Mills & Son, optician and jeweller, though he lived at 25 College Road.

Frederick Mills achieved some fame as he came fourth in the finals of the Yorkshire Amateur Skating Championships held at Carlton Ponds, Snaith, on 1 February 1911, even though he had recorded the fastest times in the heats. Mr. Mills

MILLS & SON
GEM & ENGAGEMENT RINGS
JEWELLERS SILVERSMITHS WATCHMAKERS
SIGHT TESTING CERTIFICATED OPTICIANS
6 Market Place RIPON.

The Shop for Regimental Badges and Ripon Souvenirs.

SPOONS WITH CITY ARMS IN SILVER AND SILVER AND ENAMEL

Goblets, Loving Cups and Match Slides

Largest selection of Wrist Watches in the District to suit all classes.

Wedding and Engagement Rings.

Presentation Clocks, and Silver and Electro Plate.

Sight Testing and Spectacle Fitting has been a Special Feature of our Business for years.

APPLETON'S

bought the property from Florence Snow, widow, and George Kendall of Harrogate, retired draper, in 1919 and continued trading there until he sold it to Joseph Angel, woollen merchant of 19 Hollins Road, Harrogate, on 5 March 1926.

What happened between this date and 25 January 1927, when Joseph Angel sold it to the Liverpool and Martins Banks Ltd. is unsure. The freehold purchase price was £2300 and the upper floors were let at a gross rental of £67. 1928 saw the name of the bank shortened to Martins Bank Ltd. About this time the mock Tudor facade was added, this being the common policy of the bank throughout the country. On 29 January 1935 the Directors resolved to close the Ripon branch, this taking place on 28 February.

The premises were put up for public auction but failed to reach the reserve. They remained vacant until purchased on 18 August 1936 by Jonas Gaunt, a pork butcher trading as Appletons. This was an expansion from their Kirkgate shop but the baking was still done there. On the following day, 19 August, Jonas sold part of the backyard to Croft and Blackburn Ltd at No. 5 next door, who in turn sold a small parcel of this land to Barclays Bank Ltd. at No .7 (14 Oct 1936). Appletons was inherited by Donald Gaunt on the death of his father in 1974 and remains in the Gaunt family to this day.

The two upper stories were used as residential accommodation by the Carter and Snow families, but in 1903 were not occupied by anyone on the Electoral Register. Kelly's Directory of 1912 lists a Charles Grundy dentist there, while the 1922, 1927 and 1936 directories show a dentist named J.H. Robson of Harrogate using the first floor as a surgery on Thursdays only. He is thought to have died about 1945 and his practice was taken over by a Mr. Kershaw for 4 or 5 years. In April 1956 Moon & Mallett bought the practice from Mr. Kershaw and remained there until they moved to Finkle Street in 1963. From then it was used by Michael Benson, accountant, and by Miss Atkinson, accountant. Finally since 1988 it has been used again as a dental surgery by Mr. M.B.S. Bradley. Mr. Donald Gaunt stated that from before 1937 to about 1945 Mrs. Tudor-James had the second floor flat, with her bedroom in the attic. These floors have remained vacant since that date.

Tony Place

6. *A busy scene of 1853.*

37

7 Market Place (East)

Since the earliest document definitely connected with this property is a deed of 1798 its earlier history must remain a matter of conjecture based on what is known of neighbouring properties.

Research into these suggests that the future No. 7 may have originally been part of a larger property of which No. 6 was the other section. By this theory the original burgage owned by George Pulleine (d.1619) was divided into two houses. This could have been in Pulleine's lifetime because he left Market Place properties to each of his daughters. The younger of these, Mrs Anne Chaytor, is shown in the Hearth Tax list (1672) as occupying a property near to that occupied by George Underwood her elder sister's son, who was in the future No. 6. This would not have prevented the acquisition in 1709 of both houses, still termed one burgage, by Charles Oxley.

The will of Charles Oxley the Younger drawn up in 1752 also supports the theory of two houses as it makes clear that he owned more than one house and these were next door to each other. His heir is to inherit not only the house in the Market Place in which he, the testator, lives, but also the adjoining premises at that time occupied by Mrs. Chambers and Mrs. Braithwaite. In the available property surveys these houses can only be accounted for by assuming some division of the original property. It was Charles' heir, Christopher Braithwaite/Oxley, who in 1798 sold the future No. 7 to Thomas Terry.

Thomas Terry had started business as a grocer but from 1785 had combined that trade with banking when he entered into partnership with Dr. William Harrison, who was now his next door neighbour, to found the first Ripon based bank. Terry was also involved in public life becoming Mayor in 1793-4 and 1809-10. When he died in 1811 the Market Place property together with the grocery business and his banking partnership passed to his son, Joseph Beevers Terry, also Mayor in 1818 and 1830.

On Joseph Beevers Terry's death the property was acquired by the remaining partners in the banking business, the heirs of Dr. Harrison. At that time the bank, whose London agents were Willis, Percival & Co., was allowed to issue notes up to the value of

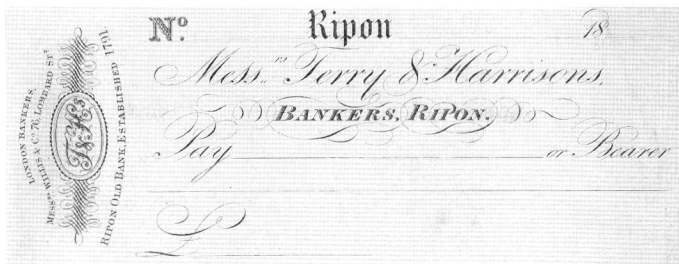

£21,825. Its property was soon acquired by Bradford Old Bank. In 1907 the Bradford Old Bank amalgamated with the Birmingham and District Counties Bank to form the United Counties Bank, which in its turn amalgamated in 1916 with Barclay and Co. soon to be known as Barclays Bank Ltd.

Although after the death of Joseph Beevers Terry the premises were mainly used for banking business they also provided a residence for the bank's manager. Perhaps the most notable of these was Thomas Askwith who had begun his career with Harrison and Terry in the 1830s. Askwith was manager for over 25 years. In 1871 he was appointed City Treasurer and also acted as Treasurer to the Ripon Board of Guardians and Secretary to the Ripon Savings Bank. On his death in 1888 he was succeeded both as Bank Manager and City Treasurer by Percy L. Fison. A recent Manager of the Bank, Mr .B. Kay, became Mayor of Ripon in 1998.

Jean Denton

7. *The Town Hall* en fête *during the 1886 Millenary Festival, with the Unicorn omnibus conspicuous in the foreground.*

8/9 Market Place (East)

These premises were once one burgage owned in the early 17thC by William Markenfield by whom it was conveyed in 1635 to Nicholas Kitchin, grocer. Kitchin was Mayor of Ripon in 1645 and 1658, but was ejected from the Corporation after the restoration of the monarchy in 1660.

The property passed to his son William, and then to William's daughter Elizabeth, being for a time occupied by Cuthbert Chambers, apothecary, who in 1675 was holding, for the first of his four times, the office of Mayor of Ripon.

No record of the property has been found for the next thirty years but by 1709 it was owned by Edward Ridsdale an attorney, and it was passed down through his family until 1782. In that year Christopher Ridsdale who was living in London sold the property to Dr William Harrison, one of the founders of Harrison and Terry's Bank. After Dr Harrison's death the property was occupied by his widow, and after her death was sold in 1842 for £830 to Joseph Beevers Terry, son of her husband's former partner, who lived next door.

After only 7 years Terry conveyed the property to Cuthbert Bridgewater of Preston whose nephew Thomas occupied it until the 1860s. Census returns described Thomas on one occasion as a miller and later as a merchant, and his wife as a lace dealer. By 1871 Thomas had gone and the property was divided into two, the southernmost (No. 8) being then occupied by Frederick Barwick, game-dealer, and

THE *Clothes* CONNECTION

the northernmost (No. 9) by Jane Bucktrout, manager of a boot shop, who had been replaced by 1881 by Thomas Pybus, sadler.

In 1882 the heirs of Cuthbert Bridgewater sold the whole property to Frederick Barwick for £500. The Barwicks continued to own the property until 1919, with first Frederick's widow and then his son George continuing with the game dealing at No. 8. Meanwhile in No. 9 Pybus was followed by William Tunstall, butcher, and early in the 20thC by Salter and Salter Ltd., boot retailers.

In 1919 Salter and Salter bought the property from George Barwick's heirs for £2,670, letting No. 8 first to Trigg and Bolton who had taken over the Barwick business, then in 1931 to the United Automobile Services Ltd. who used it as a booking and enquiry office. In 1945 United Automobile Services bought the whole property from Salter and Salter, and under the name of Caldaire (North East) Ltd. they still owned the property in the 1990s when plans were put forward involving Nos. 8/9 in a development complex that included a new bus station, shopping mall and public library east of the Market Place. Meanwhile the two shops have been occupied by a number of different businesses.

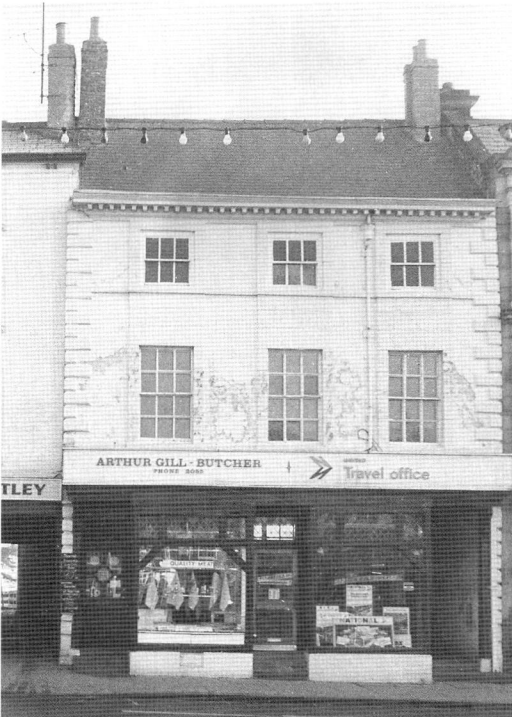

Jean Denton

8. *The Square in winter, probably in the early 1890s. The Russian Crimean War cannon and the drinking fountain were to be removed in 1896.*

9. A livestock market, probably in the early 1890s, with the cobbled surface of the Square clearly on view. It was to be concreted over in 1900.

10 Market Place (East)

Sir John Mallorie (d.1655) probably inherited this burgage from his father Sir William Mallorie in 1645. Sir John's widow, Lady Mary Mallorie, sold the property after his death to Michael Oldfield on 1st May 1656. Two months later Michael died, leaving it to his 9 year old daughter Charity and 11 year old Susannah Green, probably his neice. Charity married Jeffrey Theakston, whilst Susannah married Richard Shaw (1664), and then on the latter's death in 1672 married Alderman James Dobby. The Burgage Survey tells us that in 1675 James and Susannah Dobby and Jeffrey and Charity Theakston were the joint owners of the future No.10, but later Susannah Dobby became the sole owner.

Susannah Dobby's husband James died in 1686. In her will of 1717 she left the burgage to her three daughters, with their husbands as executors: Deborah and William Shaw, Elizabeth and Henry Green, Susannah and Christopher Hunton (a saddler who became Mayor in 1719/20).

However, Christopher Pearson, barber and peruke maker, gradually acquired all three parts of the property as they were inherited by grandchildren of Susannah - in 1728 from William Shaw, in 1734 from William and Ursula Scofield, and in 1737 from James Hunton. Christopher Pearson had been dwelling there since at least 1728 with John Inman, and they are both mentioned in the deeds of 1734 and 1737. The Average Award of 1747 names Christopher Pearson, and it must be assumed that he remained there for the rest of his life. His will of 1768 was proved in March 1772 when he left the property to his nephew Christopher Thompson, also a peruke maker.

The property was 'largely rebuilt' before 1783 by Christopher Thompson, who took out a mortgage in 1779 'to cover debts', probably in connection with this rebuilding. James Simpson was a tenant in 1783 in this four-storey Georgian property with its arched coach entrance on the south side. By 1787 Christopher Thompson, Gent., was living at Melmerby and the tenant was George Snowden, grocer and linen draper, and his wife Ann. In 1788 George Snowden sold the lease for one year to Horner Reynard, who in turn sold it five months later to John Groves of Dishforth, who in 1793 sold it for £940 to Abraham Bowerbank, late of Melmerby but now a tenant with Margaret Turkington. In March 1797 John Groves' widow Esther was

involved in the sale of the property by Abraham Bowerbank innkeeper and his wife Ann to John I'Anson, who also owned the Black Bull. Humphrey's survey of 1800 lists John I'Anson there in a burgage house and yard, and it is not until 1813 that a mortgage deed mentions an inn on the site, when Enoch Atkinson, maltster, dealer in wines and spirits, is stated as being at the Norfolk Arms. Enoch Atkinson, innkeeper, was a 'foreigner' admitted to Ripon in 1809, which suggests that the building was being used as an inn by this date, as does the coach entrance of c.1779 and the tenancy of Abraham Bowerbank in 1793.

In March 1813 John I'Anson died and left it to his daughter Dorothy, who was married to John Coates solicitor of Ripon. John and Dorothy Coates sold it to their tenant Enoch Atkinson for £1800 on 13 May 1813. A deed of 1822 mentions newly erected brewhouses, granaries, stables and conveniences behind and adjoining the burgage, also copper vats, brewing vessels and utensils.

On 12 February 1825 Elizabeth Sophia Lawrence bought the Norfolk Arms for £2300 from Enoch Atkinson, retaining him as manager. However in 1826 his widow paid the rent. In the 1860s it was known as 'Proctor's Commercial and Family Hotel' but by 1871 had become the 'Studley Royal'. It remained in the ownership of the Studley Royal family for many years. In June 1898 the Marquess of Ripon offered it for sale at auction together with the Royal Oak, Kirkgate, but both properties were withdrawn, at £3075 and £2950 respectively. However, the ownership was soon to change.

A survey of inns in 1901 conducted by the Justices for the City of Ripon revealed that the owners were now Tetley & Sons Ltd. of Leeds. The licensee was W.H. Knowles who resided on the premises. There were ten bedrooms, seating for 130 diners, night accommodation for 28 horses, a coach-house, and a good large open yard for vehicles. Still described as a 'Family and Commercial Hotel', the public entrance was under the archway from the Market Place.

However, by 1986 the 'Studley Royal' had closed. In April 1989 Allied Breweries Developments Ltd granted a 25 year lease to Northern Electric who shortly after moved from their former premises in North Street. Around 1993 the Brewery sold its freehold investment to Scottish Life Assurance Company. In April 2000 Northern Electric closed and the property has now become an Edinburgh Woollen Shop.

Tony Place

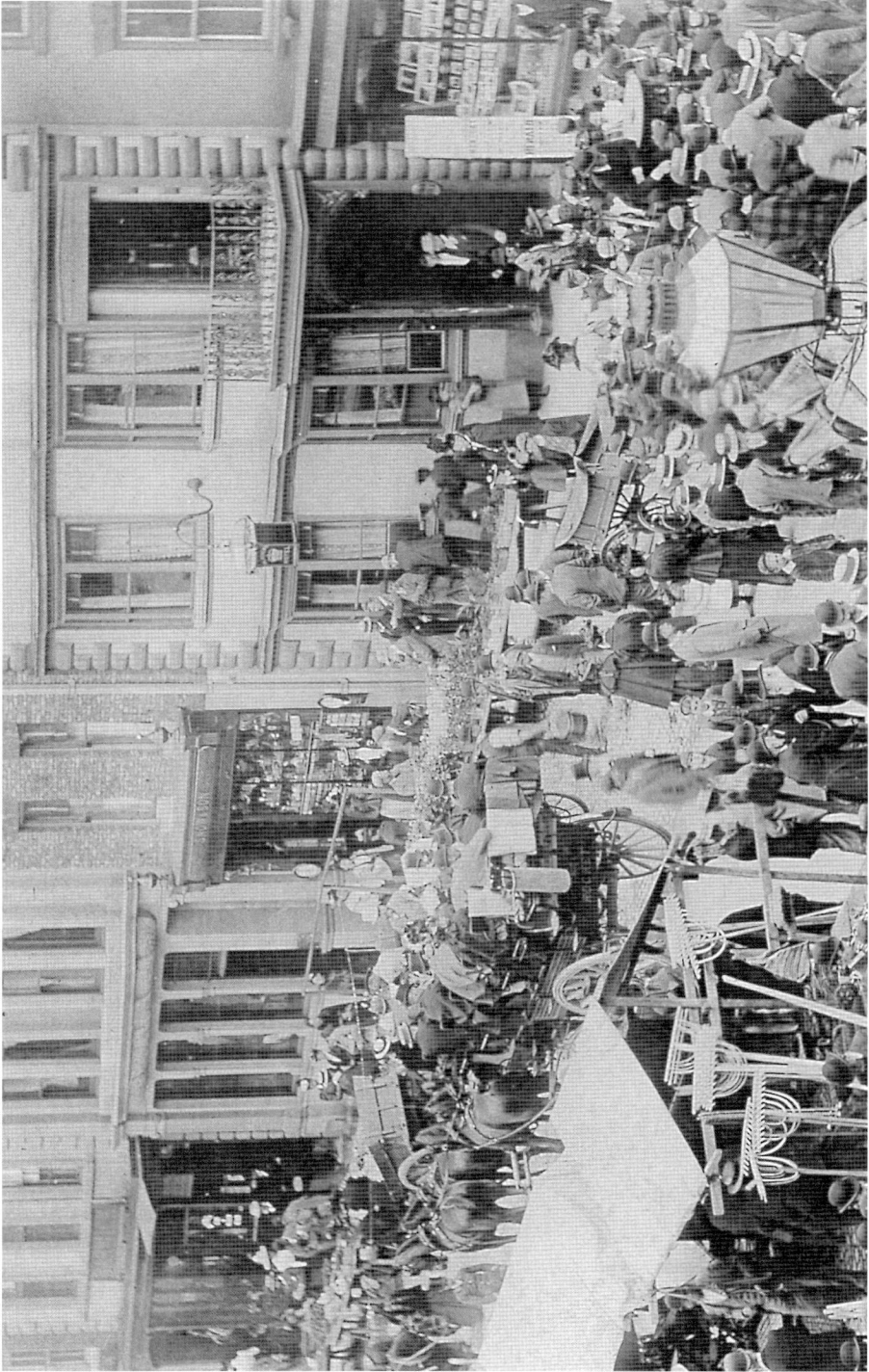

10. *A hat for every head ! Stalls, horse-drawn cabs and the Rocket charabanc on a busy market day probably in the 1890s.*

11 & 12 Market Place (East)

The earliest reference which could be found to this property was in the Vyner documents which mentioned an Anthony Middleton, gentleman, as the owner or occupier on 15 March 1609. The Middletons had been in Ripon for generations. Richard de Middleton and his wife had been resident in the 'Markettsteed in Rypon' in 1379, another had been a lime-burner in 1399. There had been a butcher in 1532, a Wakeman in 1540 and a brewer and Wakeman in 1597. However, there is no evidence to show where they lived or where they worked.

Thomas Wright is the next known owner. He was born in 1595 and had twin daughters, Elizabeth and Margaret in 1632. By 1661 it belonged to Thomas Rounthwaite (grocer, and Mayor 1649-50) and others, from whom it passed in that year to Thomas Barker of Topcliffe Manor and then in 1670 to Edward Place. Captain Edward Place, of Canswick Park, Thornton Watlass, Master of the Hospital at Well, had been very active on the parliamentary side in the Civil War. He died c.1699 and ownership of the market place property passed to his son, Sir Thomas Place (d.1729), and then to Thomas' son the Rev. Edward Place (see below).

Meanwhile John Strother, Mayor in 1681/2, had been in occupation of the property at the time of the Burgage Survey of 1675, but by 1707 Elizabeth Wilson and Marmaduke Waine were in possession, and then Richard Hinde, gentleman, by 1728.

The Average Award of 1747 gives the owner as the Reverend Edward Place of Well, and the house was then occupied by the widow Storzaker. Edward Place had been born on 13 April 1691, married Mrs Mary Peirse of Bedale in 1714, and was buried in Well on 10 May 1775. He was instituted Rector of Bedale on 20 March 1731 and installed as Dean of the Collegiate Church of Middleham in 1742, but resigned as such in favour of his son, the Reverend Edward Place (junior) in 1754.

The Rev. Edward Place (senior) had been buying property in the Ripon area since at least 1727, but the Registry of Deeds in Wakefield reveals that in 1752 he had sold much of it in Ripon, Bondgate, Aismunderby, Clotherholme, Killinghall and Kirk Deighton to John Raper of Lincoln's Inn, London, and his brother Thomas Raper, attorney of Bedale. A second

son, the Reverend Marwood Place, Fellow of Trinity College Cambridge, is mentioned in these documents.

However, yet another Vyner document of 2 June 1757 clearly states that the (Market Place) house still belongs to Mr. Place, it was formerly in the occupation of Christopher Mayne grocer, but lately in the occupation of Arthur Horsman butcher.

On the death of the Rev. Edward Place senior in 1775, the property passed to his son, the Rev. Edward Place junior. This son had been baptised on 14 November 1726 and is referred to as the owner in 1779 when the property was in the occupation of John Bell butcher and Joseph Turkington as tenants. By 1794 there is no mention of Joseph Turkington.

Humphries' Survey of 1800 lists James Bellerby as having the burgage. He was the illegitimate son of Margaret Bellerby of Bondgate. He was baptised on 27 October 1765 and married Elizabeth Johnson on 16 January 1786. They had a stillborn child in 1787 and a son James baptised on 15 August 1789. James Bellerby was admitted a Freeman of Ripon in 1805 which would have been necessary to enable him to carry on his trade as a staymaker as he had been born in Bondgate, not Ripon. A Vyner document of 1813 refers to the property as 'late of James Bellerby, now of Mr. Auton'. Baines Directory (1822) lists a Richard Auton grocer but does not state where he lived.

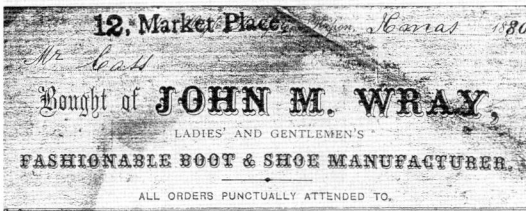

12. Market Place

Bought of **JOHN M. WRAY**,

LADIES' AND GENTLEMEN'S

FASHIONABLE BOOT & SHOE MANUFACTURER.

ALL ORDERS PUNCTUALLY ATTENDED TO.

The 1833 list of electors shows William Barugh, grocer, in occupation and the 1841 census shows that he was still there, now aged 30, unmarried, with two young girls, Isabella (10) and Margaret (8) Horsman. Presumably they were his relatives and no doubt descendants of the Arthur Horsman who had been in occupation in 1757.

At some point between 1813 and the 1841 census, the building was split into two separate sections, now known as Nos.11 and 12. I propose to deal with No.12 first as it had a comparatively short life before becoming just a doorway leading to the premises above.

The first indication that there were in fact two properties on the site comes with the 1841

census which listed a household as follows: Mary Butterfield, aged 20, head of household; Elizabeth Butterfield, aged 20, independent; Ann Hebden, aged 20, servant; and Christopher Long, aged 15, draper.

By 1851 the site was occupied by Richard Thompson, gardener, and his wife Anne who was a milliner. Sometime between 1861 and 1871 Richard Thompson died, as Anne is described as a widow in the census of 1871. In 1881 a bootmaker called John Michael Wray was in occupation.

In 1909 J.M.Wray's son took over the business when his father retired at the age of 70 and sometime after moved down to North Street. A photograph shows J.H. Awmack Ltd., china and glass merchant at No.12 but by 1917 W.B. Moss and Sons had established a dairy on the site. Moss's had opened a grocer's shop at the corner of the Arcade in the Market Place in 1899.

Moss's Dairy continued there until 1955 when the property was taken over by Robert George Verity as a greengrocers. I believe it was at this time that the two shops again became one, with the upper floors as No. 12. Mr Verity closed in 1960.

On 18 February 1960 C. Margolis (Harrogate) Ltd.

Regd. Design.   Established 1853.

J.H. AWMACK LTD.

CUTLERY · DINNER SETS · TOILET SETS · TEAS & TRAYS · MATCHINGS & REPAIRS · GAS GLOBES · DINNER FOR HIRE · CUTLERY ON HIRE

Glass, China and Cutlery
—— Merchants, ——

12, MARKET PLACE, RIPON.

Local Crest Ware.   ::
::   Noted for choice Presents.

bought the freehold and opened an Army and Navy store which continued there until the lease was granted to the Burton group on 27 May 1986. They opened a branch of Dorothy Perkins in June 1986.

Before reverting to the history of No.11, I would like to deal with the ownership of the freehold of the property. Details supplied by the Burton Group from the deeds show that a G.R. Raper had been the owner until he died about 1918/9 leaving it to Fanny Raper who died about 1945. She left it to G.T. and

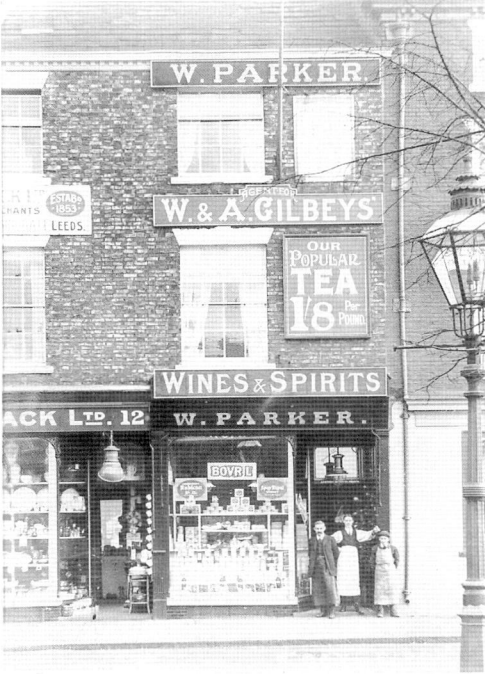

G.A. Raper, and on 1 August 1945 it was inherited by Clara Elizabeth and Ernest Raper.

As stated above, Cecil Margolis bought it in 1960, the previous owners being John H. Massey, James N. Grimshaw, Ronald Grimshaw and S. Kay. C. Margolis (Harrogate) Ltd. was acquired by Guardian Insurance in July 1989 and in April 1991 the freehold was sold to a firm in Jersey. It would be interesting to try to establish whether the G.R. Raper who died about 1918 was related to the two Rapers who were buying property from Edward and Marwood Place in 1752.

Number 11: As previously stated, William Barugh grocer was in occupation there in 1833 and he remained there until at least 1847, but by 1849 a young couple Joanathon Peacock Auton and his wife Charlotte were in residence as grocers. They were only there for a few years being followed in 1853 by William Wiseman grocer who had been in Queen Street before this. William died shortly before 1881 and his widow Ann Wiseman continued in the business until she sold it to William Parker and Son, grocers, in May 1889.

They remained there until they sold it to Robert George Verity in 1955. There had been grocers on the site since at least 1833 and an advertisement in the Ripon Gazette of 28 October 1926 makes the claim that W. Parker and Son, grocers, had been established since 1815, though whether this refers to the name or the occupation is not clear.

Tony Place.

11. A livestock market, probably 1894.

12. A livestock fair, probably 1894.

13 Market Place (East)

In the mid-17thC this burgage property had been in the possession of members of the Atkinson family. It was then acquired by William Darby as a result of his marriage to Juliana Atkinson, and in 1658 the Darbys sold it to Charles Catton whose son George held it in 1675. George was a draper and was Mayor in 1685-6, but died in office.

Unfortunately George Catton's will has not been found nor has any record of his selling the property. The next we hear of it is in a deed of 1717 relating to the property to the north where its neighbour to the south is said to be in the possession of George Palliser, innkeeper. The Average Award of 1747 confirms the Palliser ownership, but in that same year George and Francis Palliser, described as yeomen of Kirby Wiske, sold the property to Richard Ullithorne who already owned the property to the north (No.14). The inn was known as the Golden Fleece and was held by George Meek.

Richard Ullithorne died in 1752 and as a result the property passed to his only son, also called Richard and also a tallow chandler. In 1771 this second Richard Ullithorne sold it to Robert Arnold, grocer. At that time the property was

occupied by Elizabeth Ullithorne, Richard's mother, and James Robinson innkeeper. By 1777 Arnold himself was sharing the property with John Wilson, innkeeper. This association of shopkeeper owner and innkeeper tenant was to last for over 100 years.

In 1794 Elizabeth Arnold, widow, sold the property to Peter Wright, mercer, in a deed which also mentions John Wilson, innkeeper, as a recent occupant.

In 1822 Peter Wright and Son are listed as both drapers and wine and spirit merchants, a dual business that was also to last for some time. Peter Wright was Mayor of Ripon in 1807-8 and 1820-2. He died in 1825 leaving the Market Place property to his widow Ann. Their son Thomas, also combined the business of mercer with that of wine and spirit merchant, and was still

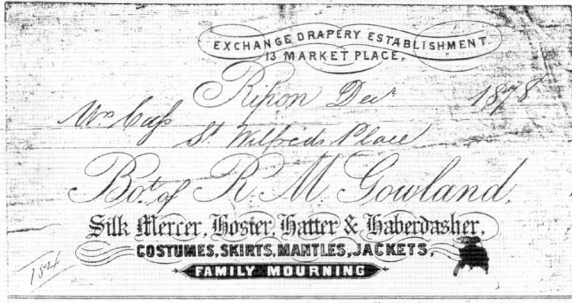

occupying the property in 1851. He had been Mayor in 1839-40. Thomas retired to Redcar in the early 1850s and therefore does not appear in an 1855 directory. Later census returns show the house and shop occupied by John Gricewood, draper (1861), Thomas Latimer, draper's shopman (1871), and Richard Gowland, draper (1881).

The public house to which access was gained by a yard at the side of the premises was now known as the 'Queen's Head'. Licensees as given in directories and census returns were as follows:-

1820s	William Burns	1834	George Fountain
1837	John Thackwray	1841	John Dobby
1848	Robert Todd	1850s	Joseph Lowley
1861	John Fountain	1867	Mrs Elizabeth Fountain
1870s	Thomas Wilson		

Census returns also reveal a number of cottages in the Queen's Head Yard.

The gap in our knowledge of the ownership of the property after 1825 ends in 1884 when the then owners, Knaresborough and Claro Bank, sold it to John Gricewood, the shop having recently been occupied by Richard Matthias Gowland and the public house by William Crossley. Gricewood now ran two drapers' shops in the Market Place, at No. 13 and at No. 25. In 1899 however his son Herbert leased No. 13 to Taylor's Drug Company Ltd. and in 1908 Taylors bought the property for £1900. By then the public house had been closed.

Taylors owned No.13 until 1978 when it was sold to George Oliver (Footwear). In 1986 it was purchased by English and Overseas Properties Ltd with W.H. Smith, booksellers and stationers, as parties in the deed. In the following year the property, still leased by W.H. Smith, was purchased by Staffordshire County Council.

Jean Denton.

13. *A boxing exhibition attracting many spectators. Probably 1894.*

14 & 15 Market Place (East)

Originally Nos.14 and 15 were one property, but as the structural details make clear, the division into two units had already taken place by the time that the property was rebuilt in brick, with No.14 giving up some of its floor space to provide access (in the form of the surviving passageway) to what became known in Victorian times as Greaves' Court.

The original burgage was owned in 1609 by members of the Thompson family, one of whom named James may have been the James Thompson who was Mayor in 1620-1 and 1633-4, and who presented a Bible to the Minster Library in 1613. In 1609 however the property was sold to Edward Kirkby, Mayor 1621-2. In 1624 Edward passed on the property to his youngest son Robert on the occasion of his marriage. In 1652 Robert sold the property to Henry Topham who held it until 1677 when he conveyed it to his daughter Faith Hepton, described as innkeeper, for £120, which sum was stated to be needed to pay her father's debts. Before long Faith's husband died and she remarried, this time to Henry Gilling of Marton Moor, and so the property came into the possession of the Gilling family.

In 1706 the Gillings leased it for eleven years to John Ullithorne, tallow chandler, who was apparently already occupying the property described as 'at the Sign of the Crown'. A year later the Gillings sold it for £205 to John Aislabie of Studley Royal, who then entered into an arrangement with Arthur Ingram of York for what was probably a long lease which would not interfere with Ullithorne's shorter one. These long leases, sometimes for 3000 years, seem to have been a common practice for Aislabie who could thus retain the freehold and with it the burgage rights, cheaply.

However, with Ingram's death, his son disposed of the property to Francis George of Barrowby who soon sold the lease back to Aislabie.

John Ullithorne's shorter lease would just about have ended and he was apparently in a position now to buy the long lease himself which he did in 1717 for £180. Some seven years previously he had already improved the property by building a cellar there, and it would seem that the general rebuilding into two separate

dwellings took place under Ullithorne at about this time. Hence from this point it is necessary to deal with the two properties separately, but it must be remembered however that the Studley Estate still held the freehold of both, which explains why the Average Award of 1747 states that William Aislabie owned the whole property.

This however is the last we hear of the Aislabie connection.

No.14

John Ullithorne had been born in 1669 and was to live until 1757. By then he appears to have outlived two of his three sons and in his will declared that he had little property left as he 'had disposed of his worldly goods long ago to his children as they had occasion for them'. The first we hear of the property later known as No.14 is in a deed of 1747 concerning its neighbour the future No.13, which shows that No.14 was in the possession of John Ullithorne's second son Richard. It seems that John had already handed it over to this son, who unlike his elder brother (who had become a lawyer) was carrying on the family business as tallow chandler and soap boiler.

The division of the burgage by this time is signified by the fact that Richard Ullithorne reserved the rights of ingress, egress and regress for himself, his wife, children, workers and agents to the yard and properties at the rear.

Richard now had two Market Place properties (later Nos. 13 & 14) and on his death his executors were instructed that one was to belong to his widow for life and the other was if necessary to be sold to provide for money legacies for his children. Any real estate that remained was ultimately to go to his only son, also called Richard. It was this property, the future No.14, that the executors of Richard Jnr sold in 1794 to Mary Horner, widow, who already owned the future

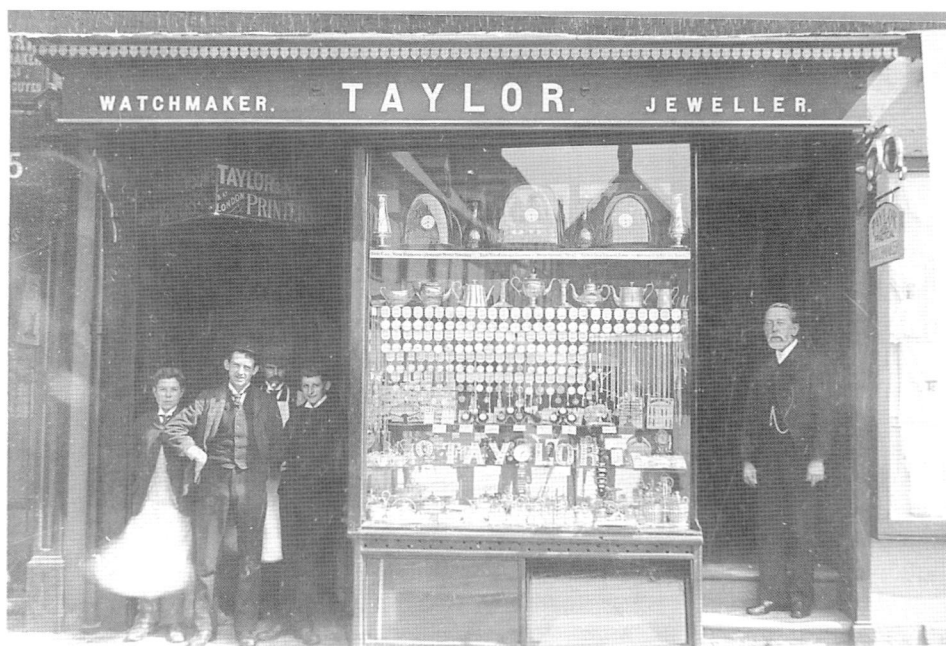

No.15. According to the deed this property (No.14) had previously been occupied by Thomas Wilks, grocer, who seems to have had some residuary interest in it, but it was currently occupied by William Horner, spirit merchant, who was presumably a relation of Mary Horner. Humphries Survey of 1800 lists Mary Horner, widow, as holding the whole burgage property, Nos. 14 and 15.

In 1823 the executors of a Mary Turner (Mary Horner remarried ?) sold the property to Richard Greaves, chemist, second son of a farmer at Birkby Nab, Clotherholme. He was already in occupation and remained in business there until his death in 1870 when he bequeathed the property to his grand-daughter Mary Ann Walbran

(see No. 15). Mary Ann lived in Liverpool and the chemist's shop was taken over by Joshua H. Wilkinson, but by 1877 he had gone and the premises were occupied by James Taylor, watchmaker and jeweller, with Taylor and Newsome, printers, in the workshops at the back.

Between 1904 and 1908 James was succeeded by his son, Henry Thompson Taylor, also a watchmaker, but in the 1920s the front shop was occupied by Miss Florence Giles, confectioner, with Taylor still occupying the rear workshop. Miss Giles was succeeded by another confectioner, Mrs. Smith, who was followed in the 1950s by Christopher Dodgshun, son of the landlord of the Studley Royal, who ran a taxi service from there. Finlays Confectioners bought the property from Dodgshun in 1954 and it continued as a sweet shop until 1982 when Cocked Hat Farm Foods bought the property from Finlays, and since then it has been used for short periods by different lessees as a video shop, a wet fish shop, a garden centre and 'The Clothes Shop'. Since 1993 'Big Bites' have been selling sandwiches there.

No.15

This was the northern part of the property the lease of which was bought by John Ullithorne in 1717. He sold part of it in 1721 to Alderman William Horner, whitesmith, who four years earlier had been Mayor. Ullithorne reserved to his family and his servants full rights of passage ('ingress, egress and regress') to the rear of the property, a right later repeated and probably the origin of the passageway known from a later owner as Greaves' Passage between Nos.14 and 15.

William Horner died in 1737 leaving the property to his widow, Elizabeth, and after her to his son Peter, ironmonger, who was Mayor in 1774. In 1770 Peter had bought the remainder of this property (then occupied by Joseph Baxter) from

John Ullithorne's grandson, another John. Peter Horner died in 1788 leaving the property to his widow Mary who as already noted, acquired No.14 in 1794, thus uniting Nos. 14 and 15 again in one ownership.

For the next 50 years only one document connected with the future No.15 has been found. This is an agreement made in 1842 involving two Baldersby farmers, William Dixon and William Wright, and Thomas Wright who had a drapery business at No.13. The purport of this agreement is not clear but the most likely interpretation is that William Dixon is selling the property to William and Thomas Wright. No evidence has been found as to how the property came into the possession of Dixon, nor as to the relationship between the Wrights, although the fact that Thomas Wright and his father Peter before him had two very different businesses (drapery and wine & spirits) might mean that Thomas was hoping to keep the two businesses going in separate premises.

However, census returns and directories show that No.15 was actually occupied in 1841 by Henry Husband Walbran, grocer, the son of John Walbran, ironfounder. He was succeeded in the business by 1847 by Peter Walbran, who married Elizabeth, the daughter of his neighbour Richard Greaves, the chemist. It was Richard Greaves who in 1855 bought No.15 from William Wright, with Thomas Wright who by this time had retired to Redcar, as a third party. (page 64)

When Peter Walbran died, first his widow Elizabeth and then their son Richard Henry carried on the grocery business. On the death of his grandfather Richard Henry became the owner of No.15. He in turn died in 1875 and his widow sold the property to Thomas Wood of Bellwood.

In 1881 the property was occupied by another grocer, William Baxter, but Baxter moved to No. 30, and No.15 was sold by Wood in 1887 to still another grocer, John Edward Parker. Parker let off part of the property to John Whitham, solicitor, and this kind of let was to continue under later owners until the end of the First World War. In 1899 Parker sold the property to William B. Moss who was also in the grocery trade, but after a few years Moss moved to larger premises leaving No.15 to Wood and Ferguson (also a grocers) who remained there until after the war when the premises were taken over by Natco Tailors who remained there until at least 1936.

By 1949 Zip Cleaners were there to be followed by a company selling surplus government stock. In the 1970s it was Addy's shoe shop. By the 1980s Sir James Hill and Sons had become the owners and in 1984 they leased the property to Taber Travel Ltd. which business was soon acquired by Pickfords Travel, since rebranded as 'Going Places'. 'Going Places' still occupy the premises. Since 1992 the property has belonged to private owners who in 1993 arranged the upper floor for residential accommodation.

Tony Place

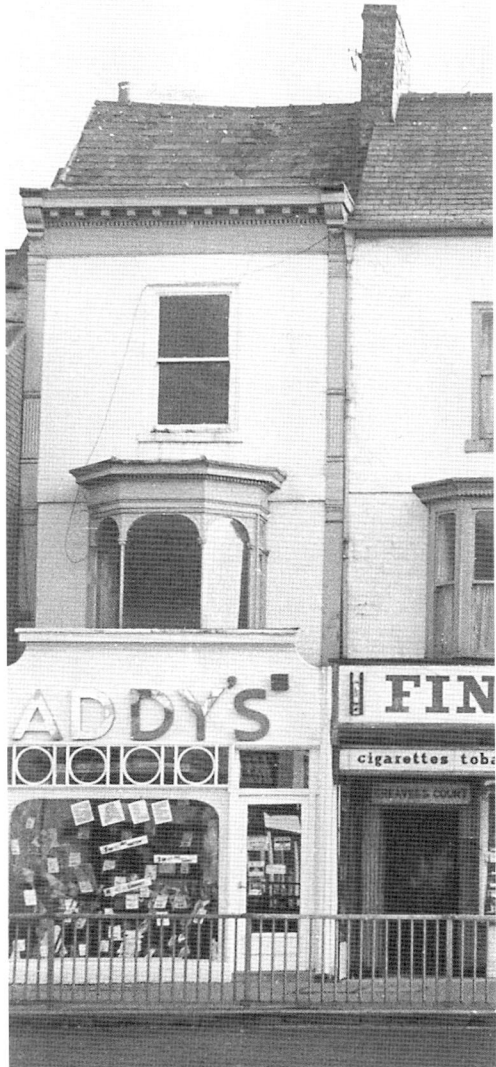

14. *July 1893. The shops have closed early and the church youth groups gather in the Square to celebrate the wedding of the Duke of York and Princess Mary of Teck (later George V and Queen Mary). Mayor Parkin and church leaders in the foreground look up at the Town Hall.*

15. *July 1893. The same event.*

16 Market Place (North)

No.16 stood at the southern or Market Place end of the block of buildings that once stretched down the middle of the present Queen Street. To the east was the original Queen Street once known as Ratten Row, and to the west was Middle Street, once the Flesh Shambles. No.16 was unique in the Market Place because it was a copyhold property and because of this it poses problems for researchers. It does not appear in the Burgage Survey of 1675 nor in the West Riding Registry of Deeds which is concerned with freehold properties only. Because none of the properties in this block had any share of the common fields or cattlegates (pasture rights) it also does not appear in the Average Award of 1747. Thus the main records available to researchers are those of the manorial court from which copyholders derived their title.

The earliest mention of this property so far discovered is in the records of the Archbishop of York's court and dated 1718. It shows the property, described as house and shop, passing from Henry Green to his son John Green the Younger, glazier. It seems possible that Henry Green was the tanner who was Mayor of Ripon in 1713-4. In 1724 Elizabeth, probably John's widow, sold it to Thomas Markenfield (or Markingfield), mercer and linen draper. Throughout these transactions reference is made in the court records to the former occupation of the property by William Horner, Thomas Bellerby, Godfrey Bellerby and Richard Browne. Markenfield subsequently rebuilt the property but in 1756 mortgaged the premises, which he was himself occupying, to Francis Spence, gentleman, of Bondgate Green. Perhaps the mortgage was made necessary by the rebuilding! If so it failed to serve its purpose because a few years later Markenfield went bankrupt and then died, and the assignees of his estate sold the Market Place property to William Cant, sadler, in 1768.

The Cants, in the persons of William, his widow Catherine and their son Francis, owned the property until 1827 when on the death of Francis, another William, a druggist, mortgaged it. It seems that this William Cant was unable to meet his mortgage obligations for the next record shows John Howard of Ripon, gentleman, the mortgagee, selling the property (described as two messuages, formerly one) to Thomas Walker, dealer in lace, for £540. It was currently being occupied by two yearly tenants, Alexander Robson and John Plummer. John Plummer, brazier and tinsmith appears in an 1834 directory as occupying a Middle Street property so it would appear that his house was behind (i.e. north of) the Market Place house, which was occupied (significantly in view of the owner's trade) by Robson, who dealt in the interesting combination of tea and lace.

By 1837 Robson has disappeared from the directory and in his place is the name of the owner, Thomas Walker, hosier. In 1841 Pigot's directory shows Walker's name linked with Severs in the Market Place hosiery and lace dealing business, and in the same year the census return names George Severs as the occupant of the property. By 1848 Walker has a new partner called Robert Aslin and this partnership lasted until at least 1875, although by 1871 no one was actually living in the property - which probably makes this the first Market

Place property to have no residents.

By Thomas Walker's will dated 1857 this property with several others was placed in trust into the hands of executors. They were instructed to provide for Walker's widow out of the rents of these properties and after her death to sell them. The occupiers of the property at that time were Robert Aslin and Mark Walker. Thomas Walker survived until 1875 and the following year his executors sold the property. Robert Aslin wished to buy it and raised the necessary funds by a mortgage.

He carried on the business there until at least 1891, but by 1897 the shop had been taken over by a draper, John Rayner. Although no record has been found of his purchase of the property, it was he who owned it when the Corporation's plan to demolish the whole block of properties between Queen St. and Middle St. was put forward at the turn of the century. When the demolition work started at the end of 1902 Rayner held out for better compensation, and his property survived until a sum of nearly £5000 was agreed in 1905 after arbitration.

Jean Denton

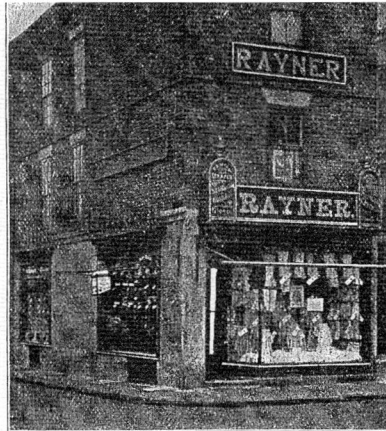

16. *A snow scene of c.1900. The drinking fountain and cannon have gone, whilst the trees (1897) and public toilets (1899) have arrived.*

17 & 18 Market Place (North)

These properties were once two burgages which in 1675 were owned by Cuthbert Chambers, Mayor of Ripon. He had acquired them the previous year from Ralph and Sarah Adderley and Hester Kitchin. The Burgage Survey states that previous owners (going backwards in time) were John Illingworth, Thomas Clark and James Cowper, Christopher Dickinson, and the earliest owner recorded, Ralph Horner.

Cuthbert Chambers, an apothecary, was Mayor of Ripon three more times after 1675 - in 1684-5, 1693-4 and 1706-7. He is recorded as having given two small fire engines to the town and a large gilt bible for the use of the Mayor at his inauguration.

Chambers' property was bequeathed to his daughter Mary, who had married Roger Lawrence, and their son William eventually inherited the burgages. William Lawrence was to be Mayor of Ripon in 1768-9 and one of the two Ripon MPs from 1775 until 1798, but by then in 1747 he had conveyed these burgages plus one other elsewhere in the town to Thomas Loup, apothecary and surgeon, for £400. Loup was already one of the occupiers of the properties together with Francis Whilton, Thomas Dixon and George Markenfield. In 1752 Thomas Loup conveyed the properties to George Loup (family relationship uncertain). George, also apothecary and surgeon, was Mayor in 1734-5 and 1748-9. He died in 1756 and left his property in trust for his infant grandson, also called George.

In 1777 after the grandson came of age, the property was sold to John Raggett of Markenfield Hall. Occupiers at that time were Edward Raggett grocer, John Gilbertson watchmaker, George Loup jeweller and Stephen Todd. By John Raggett's will dated 1793 his widow and his brother Edward were to occupy the property rent-free for life, and after their deaths it was to go to his nephews, Thomas and John Raggett. In 1807 these nephews, both living in London, conveyed the properties, again with the third burgage, to Thomas Jackson, tallow chandler, for £1,310. Jackson was soon having financial difficulties and in 1813 conveyed his property to Elizabeth Sophia Lawrence of Studley Royal for payment of his debts plus £200. However he then received it back from her immediately on a lease of 999 years, Miss Lawrence retaining the burgage rights and the average rents due.

For forty years Jackson, mortgagees, sub-lessees and the Studley Royal estate were involved in a complex series of property deals which ended in 1855 with the property back in the hands of Studley for the next 70 years.

The history of the actual occupiers during this period is equally complex. In 1813 these were Thomas Smelt grocer, Christopher Bulmer hairdresser, and William Turner mercer, as well as Jackson himself. By 1822 Thomas Judson druggist, and William Hodgson glass and china dealer, had joined the others. Of these the longest lasting business was that of the Judsons which under three generations of the

JUDSON'S RESTORATIVE BALSAM.
   A most useful and reliable Family Medicine, for the cure of Coughs, Colds, Bronchitis, Hoarseness, and all Chest Affections. In bottles at 7½d., 1s. 1½d., 2s. 3d.   Prepared and sold only by T. JUDSON & SON.
JUDSON'S CONCENTRATED QUININE AND IRON TONIC.
   This preparation contains Quinine and Iron in a high state of purity, and is the most efficacious strengthening agent yet discovered. In bottles at 1s., 2s. 3d., 3s. 6d.
JUDSON'S NEURALGIC TINCTURE for the cure of Neuralgia, Face-ache, &c.   In bottles at 1s. 1½d. and 2s. 3d.
CORN PAINT in bottles at 6d.
TOOTHACHE ESSENCE.
   A Local Application for Painful Teeth.   In bottles at 6d.
CHILBLAIN PAPER in sheets at 6d.
CHEST PROTECTORS, POROUS PLASTERS of all kinds.

T. JUDSON & SON,
Dispensing and Family Chemists,
Established 1812.   18, Market Place, RIPON.

J. H. WOOD

❧ Confectioner, ❧

17, MARKET PLACE, RIPON.

The Shop for————

YORKSHIRE CHEESE CAKES,
PORK PIES, and a large variety of
PLUM CAKES, etc.

family was to remain until the twentieth century in what later came to be No.18.

During this period the future No.17 soon came to be occupied by a succession of drapers. From the census returns the first was Christopher Horn (1841), then William James Horn 1851, 1861, 1871, and 1881) and Richard Ebdell (1891). By 1897 Ebdell had been replaced by James Hague, the last of the series. But in 1911 the Studley Estate indicated that Nos. 17 and 18 were to be reconstructed, as a result of which the businesses currently occupying them had to close or move.

Our knowledge of subsequent tenancies is limited by the directories available for study. In 1917 No. 17 was divided into three, being occupied by W & E Turner Ltd. bootmakers, Mrs. O.M. Gay confectioner (17A) and J.H. Wood baker (17B), whilst No.18 was occupied by Gallons Ltd., grocers. In the inter-war years and later, Turners and Gallons remained in Nos. 17 & 18 but there were several changes in 17A and 17B. In 1922 17A appears as occupied by the confectionery business of E.E. Deane. By 1936 it was occupied by James Smith & Son, cleaners. 17B does not appear in the 1922 directory but reappears by 1927 when occupied by two Misses Bell bakers, one of whom was still there in 1936. This business also included the City Cafe, a popular resort for Ripon citizensuntil the 1970s. Did Mr. Booth take over when the second Miss Bell gave up?

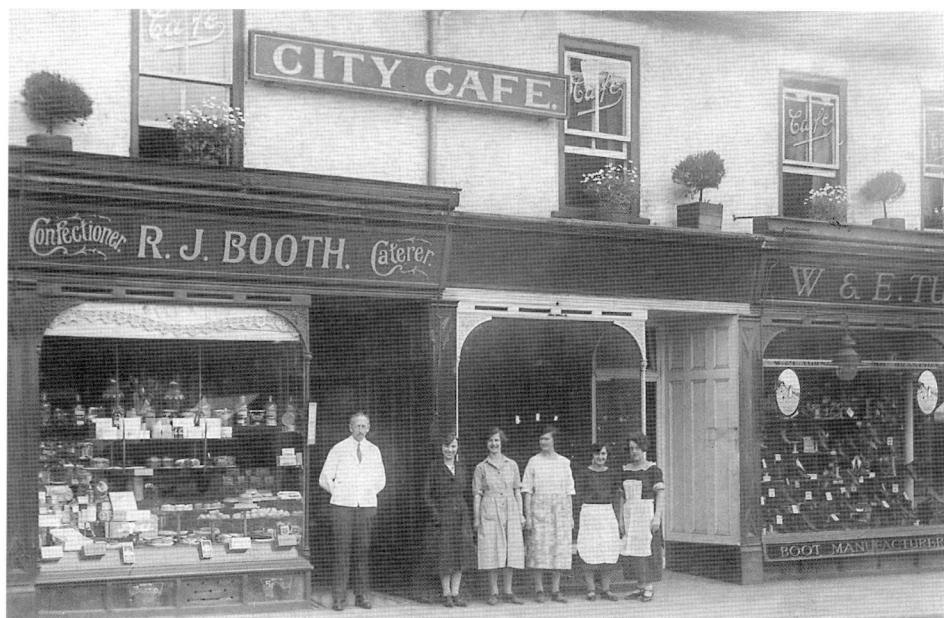

Meanwhile in the mid-1920s the ownership of the properties had undergone a change. On the death of the second Marquess of Ripon (1923), the properties were put up for sale by Clare Vyner, the new owner. Nos. 17, 17A and 17B were purchased by the tenant of No.17, William Henry Turner, for £3100, whilst No.18 was also bought by its occupier, Gallons Ltd., for £1650.

Since the Second World War both properties have again changed hands - Nos. 17, 17A and 17B are now owned by the Leeds and Holbeck Building Society who occupy No.17 and let the remaining property to Birthdays card retailers; No.18 is owned by Associated British Foods plc and occupied by Bakers Oven which includes a baker's shop and a self-service restaurant.

Jean Denton and Maurice Taylor.

17. *All the fun of the fair – including Murphy's Gondolas (c.1898).*

18. *The Cabmen's rank, c. 1906.*

19 Market Place (North)

The first known owner of this property was Miles Parcivall though we have no date for this. At the beginning of 1675 it was owned by Roger Wright mercer, Miles Stephenson sadler, and two other Stephensons, both of Rainton, yeoman and butcher respectively. Later that year the property was sold for £90 to Dorothy Dixon of Morcar, widow. The deed records that the property had recently been occupied by William Dixon, grocer, possibly her husband.

Soon Dorothy handed the property over to her son Robert, at which time it was said to be occupied by Ann Booker, spinster. From Robert it eventually passed to his second son Thomas who in 1709 sold it to John Aislabie of Studley Royal for £262. At that time the premises were occupied by Johnson Wood, grocer, who in 1711 became Mayor of Ripon. In 1716 Aislabie leased the property for a term of 3000 years to George Pinckney grocer but retained associated burgage rights. Pinckney was twice Mayor, in 1705-6 and 1726-7. The property was inherited by his daughter Frances who had married Richard Grainge, also a grocer, and was Mayor in 1759-60.

The next owner of the property was William Neesam of Cundale, yeoman, who purchased the property in 1778, from whom it passed to his son James, and from James to his son John. After this there is a gap in the history of the property although it seems that it was occupied in 1841 by Henry Burlinson, watchmaker.

In 1850 the property was sold by the York City and County Banking Company to Joseph Lambert of Ripon. In 1851 it was occupied by Robert Horn grocer, in 1861 and 1871 by Henry Burlinson again, his business apparently being taken over by John Rutter by 1875.

In 1880 the property was sold by Elizabeth Lambert to John Gricewood draper, and by 1881 it was being let to William Fletcher, confectioner. Fletcher bought the premises from Gricewood in 1895. About this time a glowing tribute to Fletcher appeared in 'An Illustrated Account of Ripon and District', according to which the skill and fame of Fletcher and his wife were such that their confectionery was despatched by

WILLIAM FLETCHER,
CONFECTIONER,
19, MARKET PLACE, RIPON.

→*CONFECTIONERY : OF : EVERY : DESCRIPTION*←

SCHOOLS AND PARTIES CATERED FOR.

Bride Cakes made to order.

HIGHEST REFERENCES.

parcel post to many parts of the country, and even overseas. The flavour of this article may be tasted from the following extract:

"It is in such places as Ripon, which are peopled largely by those of refined and cultured taste and live at a distance from large centres, that according to the laws of supply and demand, we must look for high class confectionery businesses".By 1901 however Fletcher's business had closed and No.19 was occupied by J. Hepworth & Son Ltd., the Leeds-based clothiers, who were at first tenants, but in 1920 purchased the property from Fletcher's heir. Five years later however they sold the property to the Maypole Dairy Ltd. which used the property until the 1960s. It has since been occupied by Granada TV Rentals and now by Johnson's Cleaners.

Jean Denton

19. Bryant's charabanc waiting for customers, c.1906.

20 & 21 Market Place (North)

These two properties, one of which was demolished nearly a century ago, were once one burgage which in 1675 was owned by Roger Wright and George and Miles Stephenson of Rainton, having previously been held at some unspecified time by Miles Parcivall.

By 1716 the burgage was owned and occupied by William Walker the Younger, described as a cook. Having raised money in a mortgage he failed to pay his creditors and with their consent he sold the property in 1730 to William Dunn of Thornton-Le-Moor. Twelve years later the property was conveyed to Elizabeth Peacock who later married Peter Consett the Younger of Yarm. During the period of the Consett's ownership it was occupied for a time by William Thompson, apothecary, Mayor of Ripon 1753-4.

In 1770 the Consetts sold it to John Pickersgill, merchant, who almost immediately conveyed it on a 2000 year lease to John Atkinson, grocer, for £600. However only a year later Atkinson was declared bankrupt and the assignees of his estate sold the property to John Gilbertson, watchmaker. Gilbertson was later to make money out of the Government's recall of deficient gold coins and purchased Sharow Lodge which as a result became known locally as Light Guinea Hall. In 1791 the Market Place property was inherited by Gilbertson's son, also called John and also a watchmaker. The younger Gilbertson put up the property for sale by public auction in 1805 and it was purchased for £900 on behalf of William Farrer, stationer and bookseller, who had previously been a tenant of Gilbertson.

Farrer, the author of a history of Ripon first published in 1801, became Ripon Postmaster and later a partner in the banking firm Farrer, Williamson and Co. He was Mayor of Ripon in 1813-4 and 1823-4. It appears that the property was already divided as he shared the occupancy with Stephen Lodge, bookseller. In 1820 Farrer sold the property to Elizabeth Sophia Lawrence of Studley Royal for £2000. She and her heirs were to own it for the rest of the century.

The successors of Farrer as Postmaster occupied the property as tenants of the Studley estate, first Stephen Lodge, then his widow Ann, and on her unexplained dismissal in 1832, Thomas Procter, printer and bookseller. Procter had as neighbour in the property first Christopher Bulmer, then Thomas Bulmer, hairdressers. By 1851 the Bulmers were gone and their place had been taken by William Judson, a printer and bookseller like his neighbour. Procter resigned his post as Postmaster in 1857.

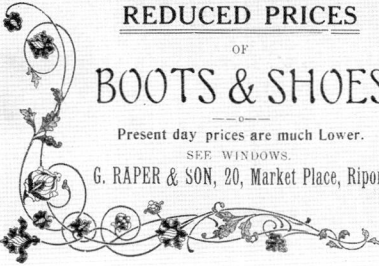

See **RAPER'S**
REDUCED PRICES
OF
BOOTS & SHOES
Present day prices are much Lower.
SEE WINDOWS.
G. RAPER & SON, 20, Market Place, Ripon.

G. RAPER & SON,
- - 20, MARKET SQUARE.
BOOTS & SHOES.
We stock the Newest Styles, best makes, including
"K" Boots & Shoes for Ladies' and Gentlemen.
Useful Children's Boots and Sandals. Rubbers
for wet weather.
"REPAIRS A SPECIALITIE."

THE "**K**" BOOT SHOP,
20, Market Place, Ripon.

G. Raper & Son, Have pleasure in inviting your attention to their first special

Show of Boots and Shoes for

Spring.
LADIES' GIBSON SHOES.
LADIES' STRAP SHOES.
LADIES' PATENT SHOES.

GENTLEMEN'S BOOTS 8/11, 10/6, 12 6, &c.

NEW GOODS! Children's Boots and Shoes

He had been let off lightly for falsifying his stamp accounts, and his daughter was appointed to succeed him.

However in 1858 the Post Office moved to Kirkgate. After this the western part of the Market Place property (No. 21) was occupied by William Eales, shoemaker.

By 1871 Judson had been replaced in the eastern part (No. 20) by William Parkinson, ironmonger. However Parkinson soon afterwards left and Eales moved into No. 20 where he was succeeded by another shoemaker G.R. Raper. No. 21 was now occupied by John Whitham, solicitor. The 1881 and 1891 census returns show Raper and Whitham continuing to occupy Nos. 20 and 21. However in 1902 No. 21 was demolished as part of the Fishergate widening scheme. At the same time Raper bought the remainder of the property from the Studley estate.

On Raper's death the property was sold for £3000 to J. Hepworth and Son Ltd., a Leeds-based clothing firm who occupied it until 1983. It is now owned by British Aerospace Pension Fund and occupied by Thomas the Baker. Thus the earliest known occupier of the property was a cook and the latest one a baker !

Jean Denton

20. The motorised omnibus prepares to leave for the Station c.1906.

21. A military parade on the Square at the end of the First World War. UW...

22. Folk dancing during the Silver Jubilee celebrations of 1935.

23 & 24 Market Place (West)

Situated in the north-west corner of the Market Place, No. 23 for more than 165 years was an inn known by the sign of the George and Dragon, and before that for 100 years as the George Inn. In 1986 planning permission was obtained for change of use to retail. The property was altered and refitted, then leased to Tiptop, which in 1987 changed its name to Superdrug.

Adjoining to the south is No. 24 which was a butcher's shop for 60 years, the last one being Dewhursts. Previously it was a draper's, before that a saddler's, and before that a grocer's. It is now Lunn Poly, a travel agent.

Records of the properties start more than three hundred years ago when they formed one messuage, described in 1675 as a Mansion House, owned by John Spence; his heirs were to own the property for another 100 years. In 1680 John Spence left the messuage to his daughter Jane who married Richard Robinson of Alne in 1684. In 1728 Jane, now widowed, and her son Richard (Jr.) divided the property, the southern part passing to John Forster of Runswick, the son of a cousin and the godson of John Spence. This consisted of a dwelling house, malt kiln, one row of buildings in the garth, the west end of the stable, half the dunghill heads and privy, half the Little Garden and half the grass garth adjoining it, free passage through the way, and an ale cellar.

In 1731 the northern part of the property also passed from Jane Robinson and son Richard to John Forster. It included the George Inn and three shops forward, three stables with hay chamber above, also half the Little Garden and grass garth, dunghill and privy, and one cellar lying under the grocer shop at the other side of the way. In 1747 the Average Awards gave John Forster as the owner of the messuage and he owned it still in 1766. Richard Bayne owned it next and left it to nephew William who sold it to John Morley in 1790, still the owner in 1800 (Humphreys Survey).

In 1802 Richard Delicate is first mentioned as occupying gardens at either side of John Morley's messuage. In 1808 Richard Delicate bought Morley's messuage and he and his heirs were to own it for the next 65 years. A directory

of 1811 shows Richard Delicate occupying the George Inn in the Market Place. In 1822 he was made freeman of the city and is listed that year as innkeeper of the George and Dragon.

Richard died in 1828 when he was 59. His children by his second wife were Richard (8), William (6) and Ellen (3). His wife was to use and enjoy all the household furniture, plate, rents, etc. and use them to support their children. The property was left in trust to the two sons, Richard to have the inn with brew house, stables and other outbuildings (No. 23), whilst William was to have the dwelling house (No. 24) adjoining, together with cottage, warehouses, stables, pigstyes and other outbuildings. Richard Delicate's eldest son Francis (31) by his first wife was left an annual sum of £20 for the term of his life.

Richard (junior)'s cousin Jeremiah Delicate became innkeeper of the George and Dragon until the former was old enough to take over, but in 1843 Richard died of consumption at the age of 23 as he was entering into his inheritance, leaving a widow Elizabeth aged 20 (daughter of Jeremiah), and a baby son (another Richard). The widow was left £20 a year in the will (while she remained a widow) and the baby son was left in trust the northern half of the messuage including the George and Dragon.

In 1843 the ownership of the messuage divided for 150 years, and it is best to trace the story of the two parts separately.

The northern part, the George and Dragon, was occupied by George Wallbank in 1848 and he was still there in 1852. Mrs. Ann Blakeborough was landlady by 1857, but in 1861 James Hanby with wife and family had taken over. Mary Fletcher (82) had moved into the cottage. In 1863 Richard Delicate (grandson of the first Richard) took out a mortgage on the George and Dragon with cottage adjoining the south side.

In 1871 Anthony Bland, then the innkeeper, was also a cattle dealer. In 1876 he bought the property from Richard Delicate, printer, now of New Jersey, USA. As previously, it included the cottage, the Little Garden and grass garth adjoining, plus stables and outbuildings. About 1881 Anthony Bland rebuilt the George and Dragon, and asked Ann Waite for another £100 to cover the cost, bringing the mortgage to £1000. But in 1886 Hanley Hutchinson and Robert Highley took on the mortgage.

In 1891 the census shows that Mary Bland, now a widow aged 60, was landlady, with her son, daughter, and two grandchildren; there was also an ostler, servant and four lodgers. Subject to mortgage the property was conveyed to John Nicholson in 1892. In the 1901 survey of licensed premises in Ripon, Nicholson was described as the owner and licensee of the

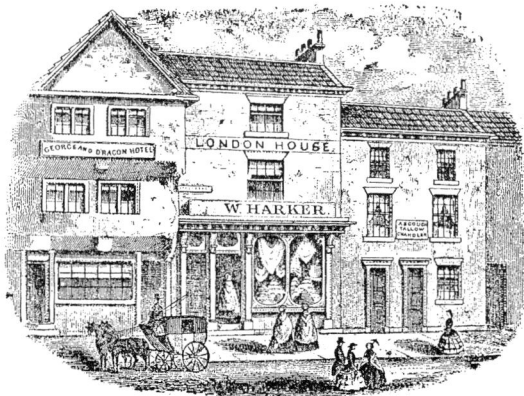

George and Dragon, living on the premises. It was a Free House and in good order, with separate Drawing and Dining rooms, and capable of providing for 180 diners at one time. There was one front entrance from the Market Place and two side entrances under the archway, which led to a large open yard with stables and coachhouse

In 1913 John Nicholson, the last of the private owners, sold the property to John Smith Tadcaster Brewery Co. Ltd., later part of Courage Brewers (1973). In 1911 the Dalton family held the licence and continued to do so until 1965. The last landlord was James Hewson and his wife Eileen. In 1975 some land at the back was sold, perhaps to provide rear access to Boots the Chemist. In 1980 permission was granted for rear buildings to be demolished and new premises built and leased to William Hill, Bookmaker.

In 1986 Courage Brewers sold it to Grantham Developments who closed it down, despite strong protests from the patrons of the George and Dragon, who organised a petition signed by 750 angry regulars. The new owners applied for a change of use to retail, and that is how it became Superdrug.

Let us now return to No. 24, the southern half of the messuage. On reaching the age of 21 in 1843 William Delicate came into his inheritance, and in 1848, then a butcher, he conveyed the property with cottage adjoining to Christopher Downes, saddler, who was already in occupation there. In 1851 Downes, employing three men, is shown living there with his family and a servant. However, by 1857 he had moved to Edinburgh, having conveyed the property to John Fossick, saddler.

Fossick, a Councillor in 1862/3, is described at the time of the 1871 census as a Master Sadler employing 3 boys. There were his two nieces, one of whom was a housekeeper. William Snowden, cab driver, was living in the cottage. But that same year, however, John Fossick advertised in the local press all his stock-in-trade for sale, along with his household goods.

In 1872 Fossick, along with Christopher Downes, now a gentleman 'formerly of Ripon, then Edinburgh, now of Leeds', conveyed the property to Peter Braithwaite, butcher, of Ripon, who in 1877 took out a license as auctioneer and valuer at 24 Market Place. He was elected to the Council in 1880/1 and served for three years. The 1891 census returns show him to be 56 years old, a 'butcher, auctioneer and farmer', with a wife, two daughters and a son (who was to serve as a banner bearer in the 1896 Festival.).

By 1902 No. 24 was occupied by Knowles Bros. drapers and silk mercers, then in 1906 by Frank Street, draper, who was still in occupation twenty years later. Peter Braithwaite continued to own the property until his death intestate in 1913, when the property passed to his widow - also intestate. In 1926 his son John Braithwaite claimed it, and promptly sold it to Nathan Cohen of Leeds, clothier, the last individual owner.

He leased it to Eastmans Ltd., butchers, in 1927 who held it for some years, latterly being replaced there by Dewhurst's chain store, another butcher. By 1986 the property was unoccupied and deteriorating, prompting Harrogate Borough Council to press the owners, Commercial Properties (part of Vesty Estates), to concern themselves with the building. A planning application to demolish it was refused after the RCHM reported that it incorporated the remains of a substantial 3-storied jettied timber-framed building, 3 bays in length, of 14th or 15th C date.

In 1991 Vesty Estates sold to Hallborough Property Ltd who in 1992 restored the building with the help of a Town Scheme grant. The ground floor was leased in 1992 to Lunn Poly and the upper floors in 1993 to T.S. Ingham.

The two halves of the messuage, separated since 1843, were reunited under the same ownership in 1993 when Hallborough Properties, owners of No. 24, bought No. 23.

Elizabeth Bowland

23. Decorated floats – also part of the Silver Jubilee celebrations (1935).

24. 1949. The presentation of the Freedom of the City of Ripon to the Corps of Royal Engineers.

25 and 26 Market Place (West)

An extract from the 1675 Burgage Survey tells us

"That John Craven (Jnr.) holds in fee simple one burgage between the burgage of Roger Wright, Alderman, on the south side, and the Mansion House of John Spence on the north side, by right of inheritance as son and heir of William Craven his father. William Craven was enfeoffed with this burgage by George Horner, Alderman, on 11 December 1668. The said William Craven died about four years ago and the said John Craven is aged about seventeen years, and this burgage was formerly of James Eagler and is now in the occupation of Mary Leake, widow".

So the earliest recorded owner was James Eagler who sold it to George Horner, who in turn sold it to William Craven in 1668. William died about 1671, the 1672 Hearth Tax returns showing Widow Craven in occupation with four hearths. Their son John, born about 1658, was in possession by 1675. Ten years later, his will (15 December 1685) left the property to his son, William Craven, a grocer, who was to inherit when he was 21; and he left it to his daughter Anne Craven in March 1712.

The inventory of goods and chattels made on 23 March 1712 makes fascinating reading. It was unearthed at the Borthwick Institute and is a valuation of both household and shop contents. Four rooms are listed in the house plus a brewhouse, cellar and shop. The Forechamber, Little Chamber, Kitchen and Little Parlour between them had three beds, thirty chairs, two stools, five tables and two chests of drawers, together with linen, brass cooking utensils, pewter dishes, silverware and a looking glass.

The grocer's stock varied from barrels of currants, casks of sugar, hogsheads of treacle, to powder and shot, brandy, quicksilver, spices, hair powder, threads, laces, pipes and tobacco. The total valuation came to £192-17-0, of which the most valuable items were seven casks of sugar worth £27.

Anne Craven married a grocer from Ripley called Christopher Burniston, but she died on 10 January 1729 and her husband passed the property directly to their son John Burniston. The 8th May 1749 saw the wedding of John Burniston to Mrs Sarah Loupe. On 13th January 1752 John and Sarah leased the burgage to John Exley, Gentleman, of

Furnivall's Inn, Middlesex, in conjunction with Thomas Heaviside of Bishop Monkton.

John Burniston's retirement plans went wrong, because by 23 November of the same year, 1752, Sarah, now a widow, had leased the property to William Grimston, grocer, for 21 years at £12-10-5 per annum. This must have been a form of sub-letting because in 1754 Sarah, who had moved to Wadenhoe near Oundle, leased it to Reverend Charles Laurence of Difford and Reverend Robert Stockdale of Wadenhoe.

Sarah Burniston evidently married for a third time, for by 21 July 1766 her widower, Reverend William Crosfield of Wickham Brook, Suffolk, had sold the freehold to the tenant William Grimston and his wife Anne. A witness to the document was John Burniston Bland.

William Grimston was Mayor of Ripon on four occasions - 1761, 1772, 1783 and 1795. It must have been some time between 1766 and 1781 that the present Georgian brick front and rear were added, and the building doubled in size. The central passageway from front to rear may well be a later modification, as a picture thought to have been done by Julius Caesar Ibbetson, and later than 1785, clearly shows a central window and a doorway to the left. The passage itself has two doors on either side, the front ones now blocked-in giving access to the ground floor whilst the others gave access to the upper floors. Humphries' survey of 1800 states that Mr Grimston owned the whole property and a Vyner document of 13th July 1820 refers to the property as being "in a great measure rebuilt by Mr. Alderman Grimston".

William Grimston was buried on 20 July 1805, having left his property to his son-in-law Reverend George Croft of Birmingham, but stipulating that it be sold and the money go to his descendants. The sale took place on 6 April 1807 when Thomas Wilkinson, wine merchant, bought it.

Between 1807 and 1811 two dwelling houses were built at the back. Thomas Wilkinson was buried on 14 May 1811 and his son John Wilkinson claimed the property for himself, stating that the will made by his father benefitting his mother Isabella, his brother and sisters, had been written in 1804 before his father bought the premises. By 26 October 1814 John had been 'fully persuaded' to hand over half the property, stock and equipment to his mother (who was in possession of it), in return for a partnership as from 10 November 1814.

It was probably at this stage that the central passage was constructed and the peculiar division of the upper floors took place. No. 25 has two-thirds of the first floor and one third of the second floor, whilst No. 26 has one third of the first and two-thirds of the second.

Elizabeth Lawrence bought the property from Isabella Wilkinson on 13 July 1820, there being no mention of the son John. Isabella seems to have been carrying on the wine merchant business whilst living in one of the houses at the rear. The purchase included the shop of William Turner, Mercer, another shop previously of Thomas Brown now Samuel Cooke, and the two houses occupied by Isabella Wilkinson, Daniel & Cass porter merchants, and George Ball.

Baines Directory of 1822 lists Isabella Wilkinson, wines and spirits, John Bland, perfumer, and Daniel & Cass, porter merchants. John Bland was still in business when the properties were given numbers, enabling him to be identified with No. 26, so Isabella Wilkinson was at No. 25, and Daniel & Cass were through the passageway at the rear.

It would seem logical that John Burniston Bland would be a link between the Burniston ownership and the Bland part-occupation. However William Grimston undoubtedly bought the freehold of the whole property from John Burniston's widow, and J.B. Bland's will of 30 November 1771 makes no mention of the property. Was he a natural son or godson of John Burniston ?

By 1833 Robert Horn, admitted a Freeman in 1823, was working there, and references to him continue until 1850. However, a Henry Burlinson, watchmaker, who had been in the Old Market Place in 1838 appears on the census in 1851, together with a Christopher Downes, saddler, who had been in Westgate in 1838. This last person was most likely to be in one of the two houses at the rear.

Following Robert Horn came William Thompson, tinplate worker and ironmonger, who took his younger son Thomas into partnership in 1871 and handed the business over to him in 1874. Thomas was there until 1883 when William E. Dixon, ironmonger, of 8 Kirkgate took over, only to be replaced by 1886 by John Gricewood, draper. Mr. Gricewood already had a shop on the east side of the Market place, but he moved all his business to No.25 in 1897. Herbert Gricewood (his son ?) took over at the turn of the century and remained there until about 1927 when the property was acquired by William Kirkby, draper.

In 1937 H. Mason, selling garden equipment, seed and pet supplies was on the site, followed by a period of office use. In March 1949 Rumfitts Transport was there, advertising in the Ripon Gazette for a 'loader and handyman', and in 1951 Lintott and Wrightson Hand Excavation Co. were advertising that they undertook all types of excavation, and boasted that they did not use any machinery !

On 28 August 1952 William Strikes Ltd., selling flowers and seed, bought the lease from William and Thomas Oliver who owned the freehold. Strikes had a 21 year lease and closed down the shop in June 1973. The following August Telefusion Ltd. took a 20 year lease but sold it on 9 June 1981 to a company called Gratispool International Ltd., Supasnaps being a subsidiary. In 1986 the Dixons Group bought Gratispool International, and in 1993 Sketchley plc bought Supasnaps.

The freehold of No.25 had a much less complicated story. William Oliver sold it on 13 January 1967 to Mr. and Mrs. Sherman, who in turn sold it on 29 June 1973 to Mr. and Mrs. D. Carr. In 1986 it passed to Mr. W. Carr and his sister.

No. 26

John Bland, perfumerer, hair-dresser and toy merchant, was listed in the 1841 census but does not appear on the Burgess Roll until 1846. This roll was usually compiled by 1 November each year, and so we can tell that he remained there until at least November 1870, but by the next census of 1871 he had evidently retired, aged 67, and the premises were empty. The Burgess Roll informs us that Samuel Smithson Hill, printer, was in occupation by November 1872.

A tenancy book of the Marquess of Ripon, started in 1879, shows Mr. Hill still there, and it continues until 1886 when the tenants were the executors of S.S.

Hill. An Arthur Hill, bookseller, was in residence in 1891, and this remained the case until 1911 when Ernest Joseph Hill, 'tenant not abode', is listed.

The Ripon Gazette had its office here in 1895 and in 1900 the printing business was known as City Printing. S.S. Hill printers were still operating in 1917, but by 1922 had been taken over by R. Ackrill, and the Gazette was being produced at 27b, behind the Victoria Cafe. It would appear that the printing business was still going on at No. 26 until 1927, but shortly afterwards the Public Benefit Boot Company was there. This became Manfield Shoes in 1961, and later Curtes Shoes in 1976. From 1977 until December 1988 No. 26 was a sweet shop called Maynards, since when it has been occupied by Imperial Cancer Research.

To complete this study, a few lines on the occupants of the upper stories, usually referred to as 25a and 26a.

Ralph Heslop was in 25a in 1861 and in 1931 there was Eleanor J. Preston. In 1936 Claude Lowis, dentist, worked on the first floor. He was followed by a gentleman called Ryles who is mentioned from 1939 to 1955.

On 1 January 1962 Ronald Albert Fisher, opthalmic optician, bought the lease of the two front rooms on the first floor, and was still there in 1971. In 1986 a company called Graffiti were there dealing in paper, cards, etc., and from 1988 it was occupied by A.J. Briscombe, Dental Technician.

No. 26a was occupied by Mr. N. Nicholson in 1931, followed by R. Nicholson in 1936 to at least 1950. A gentleman called Waterman was there in 1961.

Tony Place

25. Seats for everyone ! A 1950s view from the Town Hall.

26. *The Square c.1953.*

27 Market Place (West)

This property belonged in 1675 to Alderman Roger Wright, mercer, Mayor of Ripon in 1677-8, 1694-5 and 1707-8. It seems that the Wright family had acquired it in two sections - the northern part having been purchased in 1628 from Ingram Withes by Edward Wright, father of Roger, and the southern part, a burgage, purchased by Roger himself in 1672 from John Carlile, junior.

Roger Wright died in 1712 and it was his grand-daughter, Mary Wright, who inherited what property there was. However, the next definite information comes with the Average Award of 1747 when William Aislabie of Studley Royal is shown in possession. The property was to remain part of the Studley estate until 1898.

The earliest information found about tenants during this period comes in a Studley survey of 1792 when John Pickering is shown as the tenant of the future No. 27 which was then the Minster Inn. By 1801 William Lyall was innkeeper

Market Place, Ripon, Xmas 1878

Mr. Carr

Bought of WM. PARKINSON,

PATENTEE AND MANUFACTURER OF

THE INTERNATIONAL PRIZE MEDAL

"STUDLEY ROYAL" LAWN MOWER.

there and was still there in 1811, but by 1822 he had been followed by Sarah Lyall (his widow ?) at what had become known as the York Minster Inn. However by 1826 it no longer appears in the list of inns in Ripon and had not changed its

CLUBS COACH
1898

name since all the other Market Place inns are accounted for. At some time in the late 1820s or early 1830s the property began to be occupied by ironmongers, first Henry Morton and then in 1839 by one of Morton's former apprentices, Thomas Kendall, who was Mayor in 1859-60. In 1870 he retired and two more ironmongers followed, first William Parkinson and then B.R. Wigglesworth.

However in 1898 the Studley estate sold the property to the Phoenix Improvement Company with varnish manufacturer George Kearsley as a signatory in a deed which records one of its current occupiers as James Wright. It was Wright who had apparently already established there the Cafe Victoria which was to be a Market Place amenity until the 1970s. The Ripon Club, presided over at that time by the Marquess of Ripon, had also already moved from its former downstairs room in the Town Hall to new rooms on the first floor of No. 27, including dining room, reading room and billiard room.

In 1903 the Improvement Company conveyed the premises to the Cafe Victoria (Ripon) Ltd., from whom ownership passed in 1913 to W.A. Simpson-Hinchcliffe, then in 1922 to Thomas Leach and in 1925 to

✦ CAFE VICTORIA, ✦

27, *Market Place, Ripon.*

Hot & Cold Luncheons every day.

AFTERNOON TEAS A SPECIALITY.

Large and small parties catered for.

CAFÉ VICTORIA

MARKET PLACE, RIPON

Phone: Ripon 34

High-class Bakers and Caterers

OLDEST ESTABLISHED————AND STILL LEADING

ACCOMMODATION FOR OVER 700 PERSONS

PARTY CATERING A SPECIALITY

ROOMS TO LET

for PUBLIC MEETINGS, DANCES, WHIST DRIVES

Quotations on application

Thomas Oliver. Rights of way were reserved through the archway to businesses behind No. 27. Extensive improvements undertaken by Christopher Pratt of Bradford took place in the cafe in the 1920s. Behind the cafe were the Assembly Rooms used for meetings and social occasions, whilst above, the Ripon Club continued to have its quarters.

In the late 1960s plans were put forward for the rebuilding of No. 27 and a change in use of the property, a development which caused much local concern. Yet again it seemed that the City was about to lose a valued amenity and an ancient building. It proved impossible to save the amenity but when at last in 1975 consent was given for the conversion of the property into a store for Boots Chemist, there was a proviso that the early frontage of the building should be retained as well as the ancient right of way through the archway to Blossomgate. However during rebuilding the architects in charge gave notice that the front was unsafe and two days later demolished it. The authorities insisted that the new front should be a replica of the old one.

Jean Denton

27. *The Edwardian Hornblower, Edward Heward.*

28 & 29 Market Place (West)

Nos 28 and 29 are now one property belonging to the Burton Group but their amalgamation did not take place until the 20thC. It is therefore necessary to deal with their history separately.

In the mid 17thC the future No. 28 was owned by William Bramley, Mayor of Ripon in 1652-3 and 1657-8 but ejected from the Corporation after the Restoration (1660). Bramley's daughter Magdalen married Jonathan Kettlewell, mercer, and they inherited the property. What happened after this is not certain but it seems likely that their daughter Anne, who should have inherited the property, died without issue and it then passed to a cousin who had married Thomas Hunter of Appletreewick. It was Hunter's son who is the next recorded owner of the property, selling it in 1713 to Charles Lister.

Three years earlier Lister had bought the other property involved in this article. The future No. 29 had been held in the later part of the 17thC by William Gibson, like Kettlewell a mercer, and mayor in 1668-9. When he died it seems that his property was inherited by his nephew, Thomas Gill, and it was Gill's widow Ann who sold it to Lister in 1710.

Charles Lister, another mercer, was Mayor of Ripon three times: in 1700-1, 1714-5 and 1728-9. His property was inherited by his son John who was Mayor in 1756-7. John Lister who lived in the northernmost of the properties (No. 28) sold the other (No. 29) in 1760 to Mrs. Sarah Snowden by a deed which delineated the western boundary of the property by a dunghill which the new occupants could share with Mr. Lister. They were also to share the garden behind the dunghill and have the use of the "little house or privy" there.

When Lister died in 1788 he had no children to inherit his quite substantial properties. His sister's children inherited most of it but his Market Place property

was bequeathed for life to Mrs. Catherine Tanfield who may have been his housekeeper. After her death it was to go to John Martin, attorney-at-law. Martin and Mrs. Tanfield soon reached an agreement and they jointly sold the property in 1789 to William Bell, surgeon. Nine years later Bell sold it to John Coates, attorney, who was to be prominent in Ripon life in banking as well as in the legal profession. For many years he presided as deputy steward in the Lord of the Manor's Court.

J. WALLS & SON,
29, MARKET PLACE, RIPON.

Bespoke

Boot Makers, and

Dealers in

High-Class Footwear

SOLE AGENTS FOR

'Bective' Boots & Shoes

'Lotus' '' ''

'Brit-han' '' ''

'Dr. Jaeger's,, ''

J. W. TODD,

The Up-to-date and Central
Grocery and Provision Stores, **Market Place, Ripon.**

All this time the Snowdens had owned the neighbouring property, and Coates and Snowdens were to continue in their ownership of the two properties for another three decades, one of the Snowdens, George, yet another mercer, being Mayor in 1826-7.

In 1830 Coates bought No. 29 from the Snowden heirs, at which time it had multiple tenants, one being Ann Todd, music seller. However, three years later Coates sold both properties to Richard Terry, grocer. In 1839 Terry sold the original Coates property to John Jackson, another grocer, who in 1850 bought the other property too. John Jackson himself occupied No. 28, and No. 29 was let to James Norman, upholsterer. After Norman, No. 29 was occupied by John Harland, draper, who was followed by 1871 by Nicholas Nobbs, clothier, and he by John Walls, shoe dealer, by 1881. All this time Jackson had continued to own both properties and to occupy No. 28. After his death in 1883 the property was inherited by his son George D. Jackson, in 1909 by George's widow and in 1916 by their daughter Elizabeth Georgina Anderson.

However, the grocery business in No. 28 was taken over in the 1880s by John William Todd. Both Todd's grocery business and Wall's shoe business were to last until the 1930s. At first they were both tenants of the Jacksons, but eventually they bought their properties from Mrs. Anderson. However in 1936 both owners sold their properties to Montague Burton Ltd. The new owners

National Telephone 6s.

J. W. TODD,
Family Grocer, Tea Dealer, and Italian Warehouseman,
THE NOTED ESTABLISHMENT FOR

TEAS AND COFFEES
OF RICH FLAVOUR.

WELL SELECTED STOCK OF HIGH-CLASS

FRENCH COMESTIBLES
ALWAYS ON HAND.

28, MARKET PLACE, RIPON.

rebuilt the premises as one store with flats above, and under their present name of the Burton Group they still own the premises.

Jean Denton

28. *An artist's impression of a traditional market day scene.*

Market Place, Ripon.

29. *A nearly empty Square c.1904, before the widening of Queen Street.*

30, 31 & 31A Market Place (West)

These three properties at the southern end of the west side of the Market Place were once two burgages whose earliest known owners were William Uckerby and Richard Grainge. In 1622 they conveyed their properties to William Batty (junior) who was chosen Mayor in that year. Soon afterwards he died and his property passed to his daughter Anne, who had married Bartholomew Kettlewell. On her husband's death in 1658 Anne and her two adult children sold both burgages to John Waterhall (senior), grocer.

The two properties, listed in 1672 as having six and one hearths respectively, were inherited by his son also called John, who was occupying the larger one, the other being occupied by Francis Walker. On the death of John Waterhall Junior the properties passed to his son William, who was Mayor in 1691-2 whilst still less than 30 years of age. He is reported to have treated the members of the Corporation so lavishly with feasting that the public funds were severely depleted. After his early death in 1697, his widow Elizabeth held both burgages; she occupied the corner one herself and let the other to Ellen Walker, possibly the widow of Francis Walker, mentioned above.

In 1716 the Waterhall connection with the properties ended when Elizabeth sold them both to John Aislabie of Studley Royal, and thus began the long Studley connection which was to last until the 20thC. From this point it is convenient to deal with the properties separately under their later postal numbers.

By some quirk of circumstance during the 19thC the corner property came to have the number 31A. We know nothing of the tenants until 1760 when it was occupied by Thomas Walker, grocer, Mayor of Ripon in 1775-6 and 1787-8, who in 1784 paid annual rent of £16. In 1802 the tenant was John Britain who had been apprenticed to Walker.

Britain did not confine himself to the grocery trade. He joined his uncle and others in banking and was much involved in property deals. In public life he was Mayor in 1804-5, 1819-20 and 1831-2. He was a governor of the Grammar School and also interested himself in another educational establishment, Jepson's Hospital, the school of poor freemen's sons, and in the ancient hospitals which provided for the elderly poor of the city. In the end he appears to have overstretched himself financially and went bankrupt, dying in 1834. His son continued the grocery trade at 31A which was long known locally as 'Britain's Corner'.

When Britain's grocery business ended in the 1840s, the property was occupied for the rest of the century by members of the Moss family whose basic trade was that of upholsterer, although they frequently diversified. Then

at the end of the century the Corporation drew up a plan to widen Westgate which meant that No. 31A would have to be demolished and smaller premises built further back. The Moss family therefore left the premises and the Studley estate sold the smaller site in 1902 to the shoe firm Freeman, Hardy and Willis, who constructed the present premises. They occupied the premises until the 1990s although in the early days of their ownership they let off part of the building to others, for example John Hemsworth, the Knowles Brothers (drapers) , and the Scotch Wool Shop. The premises now house Stead and Simpson's shoe shop. Unfortunately the cupola which once rounded off the corner of the building was dismantled some years ago, leaving this corner of the Market Place with a rather unfinished appearance.

The second burgage that Studley acquired in 1716 has since become Nos. 30 and 31. Again our first information about tenants comes in 1760 when the property was rented by Christopher Lewis, and he and his heirs continued to occupy the property until at least 1810. In 1815 Mrs. Lawrence conveyed the property on a 60 year lease to John Britain, the tenant of 31A, with an agreement that he was to build two new houses on the site. Thus was brought about the division into two separate properties. In 1834 when the houses had been built and Britain had gone bankrupt, the Studley Estate took back responsibility for the property.

The first known tenants of the two houses were George Snowden,

draper, and Mayor in 1826-7, who occupied No. 30, and Richard Johnson, jeweller and watchmaker, and Mayor in 1814-5 and 1825-6, who occupied No. 31. Snowden was the first of a series of drapers to occupy No. 30. After him, by 1841, came James Fall who was also Ripon's Registrar of Births, Deaths and Marriages. By 1861 the Gowlands had taken over from Fall, and then by 1881 William Garbutt was there. But in 1883 Garbutt's business was replaced by W.H. Baxter's grocery business which remained there until the 1930s. In 1934 Commander Vyner, who controlled much of the former Studley estate, sold this property to members of the Alves family, florists and nurserymen. They in turn in 1947 sold it to the York County Savings Bank, which later became part of the Trustee Savings Bank which still owns and occupies the premises (now Lloyds TSB).

The Studley connection with No. 31 was shorter. In 1841 the tenant was Mrs. Allanson, a lady of independent means. By 1851 it was William Hutton, estate agent, and by 1861 William Tuting, hosier. Soon after this the premises began to be mainly occupied by members of the Moss family, the upholsterers, cabinet makers and china dealers, who also rented No. 31A.

When the Mosses left at the end of the century, the Studley estate agreed to sell the property (1901) to the Ripon Agricultural Association, who for some time had had offices in the vicinity. A trust formed in 1921 by this Association still owns these premises. For some years the upper floors were let to Seth Smith, auctioneer, the ground floor being used as an office and a clubroom by farmers, but it is now occupied by Jon Barrie, outfitter, and the former by flats.

Jean Denton

MARKET DAY RIPON

30. A busy market day c.1904. Note the shopkeepers' stalls down the east side of the road.

G 38032. RIPON. MARKET PLACE.

31. A similar scene, but after the widening of Queen Street (1905).

32 Market Place (South)

This property (now demolished) at the corner of High Skellgate and the Market Place was owned for over two hundred years by the Governors of the Free Grammar School of Ripon. The earliest deed for the property is dated 1616, but it seems likely that it formed part of the original endowments of the school from former chantry properties in 1555.

The school archives contain some 15 leases relating to the property, all for 21 years, although there were rarely 21 years between them. The annual rent ranged from 14 shillings in 1616 to £1/14/11 in the early years of the 19thC. The entry fine - the capital sum payable on entry - does not appear on the leases but a note on the back of the later ones gives entry fines ranging from £17/1/1 in 1797 to £34/3/2 in 1813 and later, an increase possibly due to inflated wartime property prices.

Lessees were Jayne Alaynsidone (pre-1616), Jeffrey Adamson (1616 and 1632), George Foster (1652 and 1674), Richard Rainforth (1697), William Lacon, cooper, (1747, 1760 and 1770), Paul Pickersgill (1771), William Coldbeck, cooper, (1773, 1790, 1797 and 1804) and John Britain, banker (1810, 1813, 1818, and 1825). The rapidly recurring leases between 1770 and 1773 were probably connected with the bankruptcy of William Lacon.

Of the lessees the most interesting were Jeffrey Adamson and John Britain. The wording of the 1616 deed suggests that this may not have been the first time

Adamson had leased the property since it refers with approval to his having repaired it when it had been in a ruinous state. Ripon Corporation also approved of Adamson. The minutes of 8 November 1608 record him as having been granted the freedom of the town 'for the paynes he tooke in copyeng the charter of this corporation' and he was elected to be deputy town clerk. By 1618 he had been promoted to be town clerk.

John Britain, the last of the lessees, occupied the property (31A) opposite No. 32 so must have sub-let the latter. Details of his career appear in the history of No. 31A. When in 1829 the Grammar School at last decided to dispose of this Market Place property they sold it to John Britain for £341/7/-. It may be significant that the sale coincided with a project for widening High

Skellgate, which led to the rebuilding of the property 10 feet further back, a project that John Britain, experienced in property deals, might have been interested in organising. Before this time the property appears to have been divided into two, and although now smaller it was certainly rebuilt as two houses.

The man who was next to purchase the corner property had already taken up his residence there as a tenant in 1816. He was Henry Thirlway, printer and bookseller. He bought it in 1832 and his family was to own it for over a century, so it came to be known as 'Thirlway's Corner'. Three generations of the family ran the business. Henry Thirlway was succeeded by his son, Henry Steel Thirlway, who is chiefly known now for his journal which tells us much about early Victorian Ripon. The third Thirlway to own the property was Henry Mann Thirlway who was alderman for 40 years and Mayor on two occasions (1888-9, 1913-4). When he died in 1937 the business closed, his sons having made careers elsewhere.

Aware of increasing traffic problems at this corner, the Corporation decided to purchase the property and demolish it in order to improve the view for drivers. However, because of the outbreak of war in 1939 demolition did not actually take place until 1946.

Jean Denton

Market Place and Cathedral Towers, Ripon.

32. Market Place South on a quiet day c.1905.

33 Market Place (South)

This picturesque property at the south-west corner of the Market Place is known as 'The Wakeman's House' because of its supposed connection with Hugh Ripley, last Wakeman and first Mayor of Ripon. Although no documentary evidence exists for this connection, and it seems likely that at the time of his death Ripley lived at another property, it is clear that the name will continue to be used, as it will be in this article.

The first documented owners of the property were a John and then a George Smith, but no date has been given for their ownerships and we know nothing further about them. However, in 1649 it was acquired by Henry Craven, grocer, who was Mayor of Ripon in 1673-4. Before his death (1674) he established a family settlement on the property (listed in the 1672 Hearth Tax returns as having 4 hearths) and under this it was inherited by his son Thomas, who with his wife Sarah held the property at the time of the 1675 Burgage Survey. Like his father he was a grocer and Mayor of Ripon (1680-1), and again in 1696-7, despite apparently being criticised in 1695 for negligence in performing his duties as an alderman. He eventually resigned as alderman and left Ripon for Leeds. His will makes no mention of Ripon property or relatives there.

The next clear evidence of ownership of the future 'Wakeman's House' comes with the Average Award of 1747, in which the owner is named as Cornelius Craven. The registration of his birth has not been discovered, but it seems most likely that he was a grandson of Thomas who we know had a son who died in early manhood, a possible father of Cornelius. A mention of the name of Christopher Wayne in connection with the property may be evidence that he was acting as trustee during the owner's minority. A close link between the two families is confirmed by the marriage of Cornelius to Ann Wayne, Christopher's daughter.

Cornelius and Ann Craven had no surviving sons, and on the death of Cornelius in 1758 the property passed to their daughter Sarah, who married John Roecliffe (or Rockcliffe) of Asenby. After their deaths it was inherited by their son, John Wayne Roecliffe, whose claim to have been descended from Hugh Ripley may have helped to give rise to the connection of Ripley

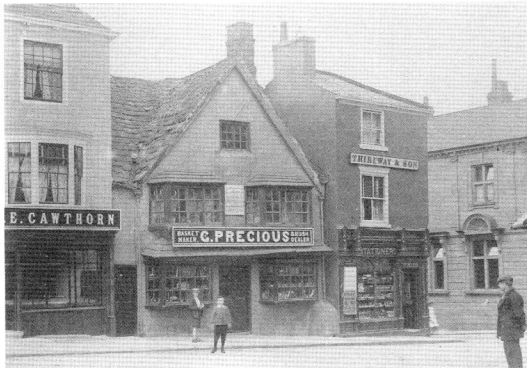

with the property. On Roecliffe's death the property was inherited by his sister, Mrs. Ann Barker of Stockton.

By Mrs. Barker's will dated 1856 the property was bequeathed to William Craven Lunn on condition that he changed his surname to Rockcliffe. It is not clear what relation William was to Mrs. Barker, or what authority she had to make the stipulation, however William duly did as required on attaining the age of 21. Apart from his ownership of this property he seems to have had no connection with Ripon. He was a doctor in Hull and well known for his work with the blind. During much of the 19thC the Ripon property was let to tenants who were basket makers, first Joseph Benson and later members of the Precious family.

In 1914 the trustees, acting on behalf of William Craven Rockcliffe under the terms of recent legislation which made it easier for family settlements to be broken, put up the property for sale, and in view of its supposed association with Hugh Ripley and its picturesque character it was suggested that Ripon Corporation should buy it and turn it into a museum. However, the property was in a very dilapidated condition and the Corporation hesitated to spend the necessary money. Then in 1915 Sydney George Moss, grocer and provision merchant, purchased the property to give the Corporation more time to think about the matter. Despite the fact that the property was in such bad condition that some members of the Corporation even recommended its demolition, in March 1917 the Corporation did purchase it together with 23 High Skellgate for £1000, with Mr. Moss remaining as tenant for the time being.

For a time after the war the building was let to a company called the Collapsidrum (makers of collapsible crates) but when William Hemsworth, owner of an antique business in Fishergate entered the Council in 1920 he soon began to make great efforts to restore the Wakeman's House and make it a showpiece for Ripon. Perhaps some of his restoration work would not meet with modern ideas of conservation, but Ripon undoubtedly owes much to his enthusiasm. The Wakeman's House became a small museum in which Alderman Hemsworth placed a part of his own collection of local antiquities.

In 1954 the Corporation in search of income leased the property to Hugh Edwards, a dealer in antique furniture and silver, who rented the front part of the property and supervised the city's museum collection in the rear room. When Mr. Edwards' tenancy ended, Harriet Jane Bourke, wife of the Sergeant-at-Mace, took over and opened a cafe . The museum was to remain in the rear and the first floor front room, with Mrs. Bourke allowing reasonable access to it and not charging more than 3d for admission. During this period a Ministry of Works grant helped to repair the property.

In 1978, a few years after Harrogate Borough Council had taken over responsibility for the property, it agreed with the Civic Society and other organisations that the building would be better used as a Tourist Information Centre, but in 1987 the TIC was moved to a location near the Cathedral and the museum was closed.

The Wakeman's House is still owned by Harrogate Borough Council, and in 1999 was adapted to provide an office for the new City Manager. A susbstantial Heritage Lottery Fund grant is enabling the building to undergo a major refurbishment in 2001.

Jean Denton

Market Place, Ripon

33. *A busy market scene of c.1905. Nearly all the stalls are set out on the north side of the Obelisk.*

34 Market Place (South)

The earliest known owners of this property were Martin and Priscilla Croft, Michael and Anne Spawton and Beatrice Taylor. In 1639 they conveyed the property to Arthur Burton, grocer, who became Mayor of Ripon in 1654-5 but who was ejected from the Corporation after the restoration of the monarchy in 1660. This property, assessed at 6 hearths in 1672, was inherited by Arthur's son Thomas, who in old age became Mayor in 1716-7. The Burton family were to continue to own it until 1756 which is the date of the first of the title deeds held by the present owners. In this deed Mary Donner, only child of Edward Burton, and her husband and son, who were flax dressers in Lincolnshire, sold the property for £150 to Edward Ayrton, later described as barber-chirurgeon. Ayrton was to be Mayor of Ripon in 1760-1 and his family produced several distinguished musicians, including two organists at Ripon Minster and (the most famous) Edmund Ayrton, organist at Westminster Abbey.

In 1808 the Ayrton family, most of whom had left Ripon, sold the property to Mrs. Eleanor Morris, a milliner, for £750. It was eventually inherited by Mrs. Morris's two daughters by her first marriage, Miss Mary Elizabeth Evens and Mrs. Ann Parker. In 1828 Francis Parker purchased Miss Evens' portion for £450, although it seems that she continued for some time to live there and carry on her mother's trade as a milliner.

Under Francis Parker there was a mortgage on the property and at some time during the 1840s the mortgagees, the

G. T. WATSON,

Fruiterer and

Florist. Tel. 66.

SUPPLIES
FRESH
DAILY
FROM THE
NEWBY HALL
GARDENS.

HOME-GROWN

FRUIT, FLOWERS, and
VEGETABLES.

OFFICERS' MESSES CATERED FOR.

34, MARKET PLACE, RIPON.
Private Address :—Newby Gardens, Ripon.

Misses Colbeck, foreclosed and in 1849 sold the property for £700 to the sitting tenant, William Thwaites, butcher. Thwaites and his son occupied the premises until 1895 when the business was taken over for the next six years by James Stubbs, although it was not until 1901 that the Thwaites sold the property - to Joseph Cawthorn of Plumpton, farmer and butcher, for £1800. How long Cawthorn traded there is not known but he was gone by 1917.

By that year the property had been divided into two, the easternmost part being occupied by Edward Cuss, then by P. Whiteley Nelson, and eventually by George Bell, all tailors. Mr. Nelson's son reports that after some lean years in which his father's more unusual work was providing gamekeepers' uniforms for the local estates, he began to win more custom from those extending the Ripon Military Camp and from officers stationed there during the Second World War. The westernmost part of the building was run as a greengrocer's shop first by G.T. Watson, then by I. and A. Cuss and finally by R.H. Whitelock.

The whole property continued to be owned by Cawthorn's heirs until 1946 when it was sold to George Bell whose business eventually took over the whole premises. The tailor's shop closed in the

117

1970s and the building has since been used as offices by the firm of Lishman Sidwell Campbell and Price, accountants, who vacated the premises in the late 1990s. In 1980-1 Mr. Barrie Price became the fourth Mayor of Ripon to be associated with the property.

Although the early 18thC front of the premises has been altered from time to time, the rear part of the building is basically a 16thC structure.

Jean Denton

34. *The Square c.1960. How the trees have grown!*

119

35 and 36 Market Place (South)

What is now one property was once two burgages, the earliest known owner in each case being Hugh Ripley, last Wakeman and first Mayor of Ripon (1603-4). However, since they soon changed ownership and remained separate properties until the end of the 19thC it is necessary to deal with them separately.

When Ripley acquired No. 35 is not known, but he sold it to Anthony and Edward Taylor in 1617. From the Taylors the property passed through a long series of owners, who in chronological order were William Burton, Daniel Burton ('haberdasher of hatts'), William Procter, Daniel Thompson, Thomas Tomlinson, William Milburn (tailor), Ellen Greaves, William Harrison (fellmonger), Christopher Barker (breechesmaker), John Stevenson of Rainton (yeoman), Richard Batty of Bondgate, Richard and John Todd (pocket-book makers) and eventually in 1806 Mrs. Lawrence, just before she inherited the Studley estate. Daniel Thompson had paid £60 for the property in 1709 - Mrs Lawrence paid £250 a century later.

Only once during this period, when the property went from William to Daniel Burton did it pass directly from father to son. Daniel Burton left his property for life to his mother and his wife (not listed above), carefully dividing it between them even down to half the cellar each and stipulating that each should provide the other access. Afterwards it was to go to his nephew.

Thomas Tomlinson received the property in view of his forthcoming marriage to Daniel Thompson's daughter. Christopher Barker bought the property and sold it as a result of defaulting on a mortgage, and the Todds, who had inherited the property burdened with the obligation to pay out other bequests, also tried to mortgage but eventually gave up the struggle and sold out to Mrs. Lawrence.

However Mrs. Lawrence soon relinquished direct control by selling a 999 years lease on the property to Edward Clarkson for £240. Clarkson rebuilt the premises and then sold the remainder of the lease to John Rawson, joiner, from whom it passed by way of his wife to his daughter and her two successive husbands, and then to the Ripon branch of the Claro Savings Bank in 1838. In 1860 the Bank sold back the remainder of the lease to the Studley estate.

No. 36 had fewer owners than No. 35. After Ripley's death (1637) it was sold to Thomas Ellis, the sitting tenant. Later it passed to John Smirke of Bishopton, and from him to his daughter Anne and her husband William Myers. They left the property to be divided between their two sons, Thomas, a cutler, and Joshua, a grocer, but in 1702 Joshua bought his brother's share for £90. However, after a series of mortgages Joshua sold the property in 1717 to John

Aislabie of Studley Royal for £170, renting it back for £6 a year.

Very little information is available about who actually occupied these two properties until the 19thC, although we know that John Terry, three times Mayor of Ripon, and often referred to as the last Ripon spurrier, lived in No. 36 for many years in the later 18thC. During the 19thC it seems to have provided offices for a number of land agents connected with the Studley estate although it also offered a home during the 1860s and 1870s for Miss Elizabeth Wise and possibly an office for Samuel Wise, a well known Ripon solicitor.

19thC census returns indicate that occupants of No. 35 were Thomas Heweton (schoolmaster) in 1851, Elizabeth Fountain (milliner) in 1861, Richard Gatenby (farmer's assistant) in 1871, Christopher Lickley (hairdresser) in 1881 and 1891. In 1892 an office was opened there for the first telephonic communication between Ripon and other Yorkshire towns.

In 1900 the Studley estate sold both Nos. 35 and 36 to the Yorkshire Penny Bank for £1700. For a long time they occupied only a part of the premises, with the hairdressing business continuing there first under Mrs. Lickley and then under John Thomas Nobbes. Even when the property was reconstructed in 1931 the new building still contained a lockup shop occupied at various times by Maynard's Confectioners, Carling and Wright's television business and later by Harker's wool shop.It was only comparatively recently that the Yorkshire Bank came to occupy the whole premises.

Jean Denton

Market Place, Ripon

35 *The market Place*

37 Market Place (South)

In the 17thC this property was the largest on the south side of the Market Place. At the beginning of the century it was almost certainly the home of Hugh Ripley, the wealthy merchant who was last Wakeman and first Mayor of Ripon, the Charter of Incorporation of the Borough of Ripon having been obtained in his period of office 1604-5. He was to be Mayor again in 1616-17 and 1630-1.

This was one of six town properties mentioned in Ripley's will of 1637 and the only one without a named tenant. He bequeathed it to his grandson, William Holmes, except that he left 'the little house on the backside' to his widow for her lifetime.

For the rest of the 17thC this property, known as the 'Black Hall', was owned by the Holmes family. William like his grandfather was a mercer and was Mayor - in 1639-40 and 1659-60. He died in office and the property, listed in 1672 as having six hearths, was inherited by his son Thomas. After the death of Thomas and his widow it passed to his sister Faith, and her husband William Chambers, apothecary.

William Chambers was Mayor of Ripon three times, in 1688-9, 1699-1700 and 1709-10. In 1716 an inventory of household effects shows the Chambers home to have consisted of a Great Chamber, an Out-Chamber, a little Parlour, a Kitchen and a back kitchen, a Buttery (with a bed in it), two servants' bedrooms and another bedroom, as well as an apothecary's shop, a cellar and stabling. The present structure seems to be the result of a re-building in the 1730s, as suggested by its style and the date of 1738 (now lost) on a rainwater head, but there appears to have been further work on the back of the house in the 1770s.

It should not go un-recorded that also in the 1730s, the Chambers family brought up and educated at the local Grammar School a distant relative from Scotland, who left Ripon in 1739 when he was sixteen. He was later to become Sir William Chambers, one of the premier architects of the late 18thC, interred in Westminster Abbey on his death in 1796.

How long the Chambers family actually occupied the property is not known but in a 1753 edition of the York Courant it was advertised to let, with a reference to its previous tenant Col. Fitzgerald. The advertisement contains a special mention of 'good pipe water', stabling for three horses and a fine terrace walk with an extensive view.

The property remained in the ownership of the Chambers family until it was sold in 1813 by Lieutenant John Milbanke Chambers of the Bengal Light Infantry to Francis Walker, gentleman, who seven years later sold it to Elizabeth Sophia Lawrence of Studley Royal. It was to remain part of the Studley estate until after the death of the second Marquess of Ripon in 1923.

Our knowledge of the occupants of the property during this period of Studley ownership starts with the 1851 census. During the 1850s the tenant was Alderman John Thompson, Coroner and Medical Practitioner, and later his widow. By 1871 Thomas Gowing, Master Joiner, was renting the property and providing accommodation for a number of lodgers. From 1880 Mrs. Elizabeth Blakey and Mrs. Fall ran the property as a lodging house but by 1890 it was Ripon Post Office, with first Henry Burdon and later William Watts as Postmasters.

When the Post Office moved to North Street in 1906 the Marquess of Ripon advertised the property for sale. It then contained eleven rooms plus kitchen, scullery, bathroom and w.c., attics and cellars. Outbuildings consisted of coal-house, wash-house (with chamber over), stable (with hay-chamber over), saddle-room, horse-box, coach-house, greenhouse and rooms formerly used as offices. A suitable buyer not having been found, the property was let to Samuel Badrock, confectioner, who transformed it into an hotel and restaurant, although with part of the front premises let as a separate shop occupied at one time by Alves, florists, and later by Harker's linen store.

After the First World War the hotel and restaurant was taken over by Mrs. A.M. Leach and then by James Grice who in 1925 purchased the property from Commander Clare Vyner of

Newby Hall, who had acquired it on the death of the 2nd Marquess. To the existing structure a ballroom was added between 1925 and 1930, and extra amenities too during the Second World War, when it was conveyed to C.G. and G. Gay under the name of the Lawrence Hotel Restaurant and Cafe Company. At what time the hotel side was abandoned is not certain but the restaurant and ballroom facilities continued until the 1960s, providing an important venue for local social events.

The Halifax Building Society, now the Halifax Bank, acquired the property in 1966.

Jean Denton

38 Market Place (South)

Ripon's Town Hall stands on the site of two ancient burgages which in the early 17thC were both in the possession of Henry Warwick, spurrier, and then of his son John. After John the properties fell into separate hands and so it is necessary to deal with them separately.

The westernmost of the two was held after John Warwick by John Langthorne and was inherited by his daughter Jane, who married George Wreakes. In 1670 George and Jane Wreakes sold the property described as 'the inn at Hollin Hill' for £250 to George Horner who was to become Mayor of Ripon in 1676-7. In 1672 the property was listed as having six hearths. When Horner married Ellen Porter, the daughter of a former proprietor of the Unicorn Inn, this property became her jointure and with her husband's death in 1679 she soon took possession.

In view of what is to be maintained later, it may be significant to draw attention to a statement in the Corporation records that 'ye brasse bushel is in the custody of Mrs. Ellen Horner' and an even more significant statement of 1688 that Mrs. Horner is owed the sum of £11 or 'eleven years rent' for the use of her parlour for the meetings of the Corporation. Now it is true that by this time Ellen Horner had acquired the Unicorn Inn and this has led to the assumption that it was there that the Corporation met, but a document of 1715 to be described later suggests that the room rented was in the 'inn at Hollin Hill' rather than the Unicorn.

The next owner of this property was Ellen Horner's nephew Luke Lathom, who sold it in 1701 to William Chambers, apothecary, who was already occupying the property next door. On William Chamber's death it was inherited by his daughter Frances, and it is her lease of it to Richard Stewartson 'inholder' (sic) in 1715 which is the document previously mentioned. The lease contains a provision that Stewartson is to continue to allow the Corporation of Ripon 'as at present and for * years past' to make use of the 'low room fronting the Market Place' as often as required for a yearly rent of 20 shillings. The asterisk is where there is a hole in the document, but the missing word seems likely to have been 'many'.

Shortly after making this lease Frances married Thomas Thornton and in

1723 they sold the property for £315 to William Aislabie of Studley Royal.

To turn to the easternmost of the two properties making up the present Town Hall. This property passed from the Warwicks through the marriage of Elizabeth Warwick to John Godfrey of Spofforth. In 1651 the Godfreys sold it to John Horner, brother of the George Horner who was later to purchase the neighbouring property. That same year John was Mayor of Ripon and again in 1661-2. After his death the property passed for life to his widow Edbura, who held it in 1672 (eight hearths) and in 1675. After her death it was to be inherited by the eldest of their sons with suitable provision for four other sons.

Unfortunately at this point we lose sight of the family. The next reference to the property is in a deed of 1717 relating to an adjacent property where its neighbour to the west is said to be owned by Edward Metcalfe. His widow inherited and by her will it eventually came into the possession of Ellen, daughter of John Allanson of Littlethorpe. She and her husband George Charnock, merchant, sold the property in 1766 to William Aislabie for £367/10/-. Thus both the future Town Hall properties were now in the possession of the Studley estate.

In 1798 Mrs. Allanson of Studley commissioned James Wyatt, a rival of Robert Adam, to design a Town Hall which would provide Assembly Rooms for the town on the site of two houses she owned in the Market Place. She agreed that the Town Council which had for some time met there should continue to do so in the new Town Hall after its completion in 1800.

The facade to the Market Place exhibits an attached Ionic portico and pediment of five bays (three with balconies) over a rusticated ground floor with arched windows. The front basement had wells and windows protected by iron railings (removed in the 1890s).

The Assembly Rooms (membership and attendance by subscription), the Grand Salon (45' by 24') with its minstrel gallery for festive occasions (the largest room in the town until the Victoria Hall was built in 1886) and gracious ante-room were reached by a fine staircase and spacious landing. The large room to the right of the entrance hall was a Committee Room (later a News Room) and with a kitchen and Card Room made up the West Wing. The Corporation not only used these rooms for its meetings but also for official dinners.

The East Wing (except for the front rooms: Public Reading Room below and Grand Salon above) provided a set of private apartments for the Clerk to the Council (who were also country solicitors to the Lords of Studley - Richard Nicholson 1819-53 and his son Richard Ward Nicholson 1853-81). A portrait of Mrs. Allanson was hung in the Grand Salon (still seen today) and after her death in 1808 a memorial plaque was placed in the Committee Room.

The Studley estate passed to her niece, Mrs. Sophia Lawrence, and then to the Earl de Grey (1846) and in 1859 to the (later)

RIPON MARKET PLACE and TOWN HALL, IN 1837

Marquess of Ripon who, except for a period of 16 years (1835-51) continued as benefactors of the City, with the City Council allowed their use of the Town Hall. The exception came in 1835 when Mrs. Lawrence disapproved of the election under new legislation of 5 Whigs and banned the Council from the Town Hall. They moved to another of the Studley properties in Kirkgate until 1851 when Earl de Grey allowed them back to the West Wing.

In 1859 a gas illuminated clock made by Richard Blakeborough was provided in the pediment of the building.

The Marquess, a staunch Mason, allowed the De Grey and Ripon Lodge the use of the elegant rear room on the first floor as a meeting room during the 1860s and 70s.

In 1880 the Corporation wished to develop the Town Hall for public offices and build a large Public Hall on the land behind. Negotiations started in 1881 when the private apartments in the East Wing became vacant on the death of the Clerk, Richard Ward Nicholson. The Council wanted control of the whole site, but the Marquess wishing to reserve the News and Reading Rooms, offered a lease of the private apartments together with the free use of the Council Room.

In 1886 as a permanent memorial of the Millenary Festival, the motto (a form of psalm 127) *Except ye Lord keep ye Citie ye Wakeman waketh in vain* was inscribed in gilt letters on the cornice on the front of the Town Hall.

To commemorate his year of office as Mayor (1896, the year of Ripon's second festival), the Marquess gifted the building to the City for use as a Town Hall. The memorial tablet to Mrs. Allanson who built the Town Hall was re-erected in the entrance hall with an additional tablet beneath, recording the gift.

The private apartments on the first and second floors of the East Wing became the accommodation for the Town Hall Keeper, and the ground floor Reading Room became the Mayor's Reception and Committee room.

In 1899 the Town Hall was connected to the telephone exchange, and in 1909 the old-fashioned open fires were replaced with the then new 'steamless' radiators operated by gas. Conversion to electricity was not carried out until the 1930s.

In 1910 all the City Council's offices were concentrated in the Town Hall, first the City Collector's office, followed by those of the City Surveyor and Sanitary Inspector. In 1932 the then Council Chamber was taken over as the City Engineers's office on a trial basis for three months during which time the council met in the Large Chamber. The arrangements were confirmed and the Council continues to meet in the Grand Salon today.

In 1933 a new clock was installed by C.H. Potts (Leeds) at a cost of £50 with guaranteed timekeeping for five years to within 5 seconds per week; a new fire alarm system was installed together with a vault with fire-proof door for storage of documents.

In 1939 the Corporation provided an ARP Control Room in the garden at the rear with access from Water Skellgate, and after the outbreak of war the main entrance to the building was protected by sandbags, the lower portions of the ground floor windows bricked up and a fire escape provided from the upper floor. The Spode dinner service, glass, silver and the more valuable paintings were stored in the strong room.

By the late 1940s there was a need to repair the results of wartime neglect. Internal decoration and renewal of lighting in the Council Chamber was carried out in 1949/50 but the extensive repair needed to the front of the building had to wait until 1958.

Floodlighting to the front of the Town Hall was installed in time for the 1952 St. Wilfrid's Festival.

In 1957 the City Engineer's Department moved to Low St. Agnesgate, into part of the Corporation Depot; the former Plan Room in the Town Hall was incorporated into the Keeper's accommodation, while the City Engineer's office (the fine room which for many years had been the Council chamber) became the Town Clerk's Office. The Town Clerk's previous office on the ground floor became a Members Room and Library.

In 1974 the Town Hall passed into the ownership of Harrogate Borough Council. The Queen granted a new charter to Ripon to retain its City status and to continue its prerogative titles. The new Ripon City Council was granted tenancy of the previous Town Clerk's office as an office for its first Clerk; continued use of the Mayor's Parlour; permission to hold Council meetings in the Large Chamber, and vaults to store its civic treasures.

Since the Marquess of Ripon gave the Town Hall to the City, the Sergeant-at-Mace was both the Mayor's attendant and the Town Hall Keeper. In 1980 the two posts were separated, the Sergeant-at-Mace and the Clerk being responsible to Ripon City Council, and the Town Hall Keeper to Harrogate Borough Council.

After 1974 Harrogate Borough Council established a Housing Office and an Office for the payment of Rates on the ground floor. The rear room on the first floor was leased to the Registrar of Births, Marriages and Deaths.

In 1994 the Borough Council provided a paved ramp, protected from the roadway by ornamental iron railings, to the front door and a lift to the first floor to improve access for the disabled.

It is only in recent years that Ripon Town Hall has received Royal visitors: HM Queen Elizabeth and the Duke of Edinburgh after the Royal Maundy distribution at the Cathedral (1985); Queen Elizabeth the Queen Mother to the Ripon 1100 Festival (1986) and Prince Charles in 1994 to open the 'Vision of Ripon' exhibition and to unveil a plaque in the entrance hall to commemorate his visit.

Jean Denton
John Whitehead

39 Market Place (South)

The National Westminster Bank plc now occupies both Nos. 39 and 40, but this merger only dates from the late 20thC; before then the two properties had many separate owners and occupiers.

The Burgage Survey of 1675 shows No. 39 to have been in the possession of Anna Spence who had inherited the property from John Spence the younger, grocer, Mayor of Ripon in 1660-61. Spence was removed from the office of Alderman by the Corporation Commissioners in 1662 for illegally granting freedoms to various people 'privately in his own house'. Such persons were now to come before the full Corporation in the proper manner to be legally admitted freemen, and future Mayors were warned against Spence's practice.

In January 1688/9 No. 39 was conveyed by Anna Spence to Abraham Brignell of Ripon, tallow chandler. Seven years later, in May 1695, he mortgaged the property to William Clarke of Wath, gentleman, for £80. Later Brignell moved to Littlethorpe and in 1708 the property came once more into the hands of Anna Spence, now Anna Andrews, widow, with John Horner, grocer, for £150. The property continued to change hands and a few years later was held by Richard Browne of Ripon Parks, yeoman, who in March 1715 transferred it to John Aislabie of Studley Royal for £200. Almost immediately Aislabie with the consent of Browne entered into an agreement with John Mush, potter, (who was already occupying the premises), for a demise of 3000 years for £190 - an arrangement by which Aislabie secured control of the burgage rights cheaply.

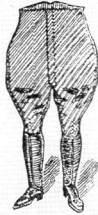

The 1747 Average Award shows it to be still part of the Studley estate and a John Mush (junior ?) was still in occupation. However, the property was soon to pass to Christopher Hebden, and in 1751 his eldest son, who was his executor, transferred it to his younger brother William. The property was at that time in the occupation of Thomas Sowerby and Thomas Raven. Six years later William Hebden, a tanner of Grantley, transferred the demise to Robert Watson of Ripon, currier, who still held the property in 1800.

In 1823, however, it was John Howard, gentleman, who held the property but in that year he formally transferred it back to the Studley estate (in the person of Elizabeth Sophia Lawrence) where it remained until 1900.

During that time the following tenants are recorded:-

1830s to 1853   Mrs. Elizabeth Coates, widow, of independent means.

1861 census   George Naylor Mallinson, grocer

1871 census   Elizabeth Severs and her son Thomas, fellmonger

1881 census   Elizabeth Proctor, Postmistress - the property had become the Post Office for a few years.

1891 census   John Lee, retired solicitor's clerk (the property was in fact being used as offices by Edmundson and Gowland, solicitors).

In 1900 Edmundson and Gowland purchased the property from the Studley estate but almost immediately sold it to John Harrison, tailor. In 1920 the National Provincial Bank Ltd. bought it from his widow who had let it to the Ripon Cycle Co. (later known as the Ripon Cycle & Wireless Co.). By the 1930s No. 39 was divided, the front part of the building being Kennedys tobacco and confectionery shop whilst the rear part (No. 39A) was let out to Robert and Frances Hall as private residential accommodation, accessed initially from Water Skellgate and by a side passage from the Market Place, but only the former entrance was available from the late 1940s.

In 1961 No. 39 merged with No. 40 to the east when the National Provincial Bank rebuilt these two properties to form one unit as it is today. A few years later (1970) it became the National Westminster Bank.

Geoff Hayward &
Jean Denton

40 Market Place (South)

No. 40 consisted of two properties from at least the early 17thC until the mid-19thC. The small western part (40A), fronting onto the Square and consisting originally of one shop and the chamber over it, belonged to the Governors of Ripon Free Grammar School. The earliest reference to the property is in 1608 but it seems likely that it was one of the original Tudor endowments of the school. The lessees named in a series of documents are as follows:.

1608	Thomas Burton and Edward Hebden
1629	Leonard Spence
1652	Alderman Anthony Braithwaite, sadler, Mayor 1653-4 (ejected from his office of Alderman in 1662 by the Corporation Commissioners' purge)
1674	William Braithwaite, sadler (son of Anthony ?)
1678	Christopher Terry, barber chirurgeon
1697	Anna Horner, widow (a shop, housestead and chamber over)
1716	Anna Horner (reference to house where shop and chamber once stood)
1735 & 1747	Alderman John Horner (probably the Horner, grocer, who was Mayor in 1727-8 and 1746-7)
1760 & 1770	John Terry, spur maker, Alderman from 1761 and Mayor in1762-3, 1773-4 and 1786-7
1780	John Snowden, barber
1790	Miss Elizabeth Snowden, daughter of John
1797	Horner Reynard, gentleman
1804	Anthony Robinson, surgeon.
1813 & 1825	James Morley, surgeon
1840s	John Todd, sadler

Some of the lessees certainly lived elsewhere and presumably sub-let their premises. There is no information about entry fines or rents before 1697 when the annual rent was 8/-, rising to 9/- in 1770 and £1/2/1 in 1813. Entry fines and costs of lease rose from £2/8/6 in 1770 to £21/16/6 in 1813.

In 1859 the Grammar School sold the property to the Knaresborough and Claro Bank, and at this stage it was merged with its eastern and much larger neighbour (40B).

In the later 17thC this had been owned by the same Anna Andrews (nee Spence) who owned No. 39. By the 1730s it had passed to John Spence, presumably a relative, but by 1747 it was the property of Margaret Myers and her son John. In 1790 it was in the possession of Alderman William Robinson, apothecary, Mayor in 1777-8 and 1789-90. He resigned his office as Alderman in 1802 but probably remained in possession until his death in 1813, to be succeeded there by Alderman John Stevenson, mercer, Mayor in 1797-8 and 1811-2.

Nothing is known as to what happened after the death of Alderman Stevenson in 1824, but at some stage the property was acquired by John Todd, sadler, with the Knaresborough and Claro Bank (est. 1831) tenants from the early 1830s. In 1846 Todd sold most of the property to the bank, and the rest in 1859, at the time that the Bank acquired the former Grammar School property (see above). No. 40 was then rebuilt as one property. Forty years later (1899) the Bank rebuilt the premises once again, this time in the florid style of the period, with a statue of St. Wilfrid placed in a niche on the facade of the 'imposing new premises'. In 1903 the Knaresborough and Claro Bank became part of the National Provincial Bank Ltd. which went on in 1920 to acquire No. 39 (see above), and sell off their other property, No. 41.

In September 1961 a demolition order was granted to the bank to pull down the existing premises to make way for a single new building. The old buildingwas demolished in 1962 during which time its timber-framed construction was exposed. A bottle containing a worksheet with the names of those who were employed in the 1899 rebuilding was found. The Bank promised to make every effort to preserve the architectural character of the Market Square and to incorporate the statue of St. Wilfrid high on the new building. The latter promise was certainly kept but whether the Bank kept the other has been questioned. In 1970 the National Provincial Bank merged with the Westminster Bank to become the National Westminster Bank plc.

Geoff Hayward
Jean Denton

41 Market Place (South)

Nothing has come to light about this property before the 1740s. In 1747 it was recorded in the Average Award that the property belonged to the heirs of Stephen Palliser. Palliser was a tanner and had been Mayor of Ripon in 1725-6 and 1735-6, and his heirs as named in his will of 1740 were in fact his widow and their four daughters.

After this, information is limited for a century to an abstract of title written in 1850 when the property was to be sold and apparently title deeds were missing. The 1850 document lists owners since the Pallisers as Thomas Trees, Mrs. Alice Haddon, Matthew Thomas Trigg and Jane his wife, and Edward Taylor of Kirkham Abbey. No dates are given and no information as to how these people came to acquire their property.

Records show that there were a number of Thomas Trees living in Ripon in the 18thC, but so far no connection has been found to link one with the Pallisers or with Mrs. Haddon, whose ownership is confirmed by Humphries Survey of 1800. Mrs. Haddon is best known as the owner of the Unicorn Inn, and her will shows her bequeathing a house in Ripon to her niece Jane Trigg, whose husband was a merchant of Sculcoates near Hull. It has not been discovered how Edward Taylor acquired the property.

Before its sale in 1850 the property was occupied by a series

of private tenants, named in the census returns and directories as Elizabeth Harrison, Mrs. H.A.M. Clough, and in 1841 two sisters - the Misses Sarah and Harriet Clough - aged 90 and 85 respectively.

In 1850 the property was bought by James Fairburn, stationer and bookseller, who occupied it for the next thirty years, eventually selling it in 1880 to his neighbour at No. 40, the Knaresborough and Claro Bank.

It was apparently used as supplementary office space and living accommodation for the bank manager. About 1904 the bank leased No. 41 to Mr. T.K. Smithson who carried on a glass and china business there until 1920.

When the Smithsons left, the National Provincial Bank which had taken over the Knaresborough and Claro Bank sold the property to Lloyds Bank. They carried on business there until 1936 when they sold the premises to Sydney George Moss, grocer and provision merchant, who had been Mayor in 1929. In 1937 Ripon's first Milk Bar was opened there. Later owners were Mrs. N.M. Struthers (1951-5) and Mr. E. Kendrew (1955-85). Then it was acquired by the Trustees of Cocked Hat Farm Foods Ltd. (Pension Fund). It is now occupied by a Chinese Restaurant.

Jean Denton

42 Market Place (South)

This property is situated in the south-east corner of the Square, marking the end of Market Place South - the adjacent property to the east is No. 1 Kirkgate. No. 42 has for many years been a jeweller's and silversmith's shop but before that was a private residence. The present owner, Mrs. M. McArdle (nee Row) is the daughter of Arthur Mallinson Row and grand-daughter of Douglas Row (born c.1870 died 1932) who was apprenticed to the Severs brothers, former owners of the business, and afterwards bought the business from them. Mrs. McArdle and her parents lived in the house from 1940 for about seven years. The upper rooms are now let as offices.

The front of the house was altered when it was converted into a shop. The original entrance was on the right and the passage was behind the present display window. The new entrance to house and shop was made on the left, and the middle of the facade was made into display windows.

There are two attic rooms in the roof. The smaller room has a blocked off inner window over the stairs and a sky light in the roof instead. Both rooms show the original beams and doors. On the second floor there are two larger bedrooms with original doors and window seats. On the first floor is the original sitting room at the front and a dining room in the extension at the back, plus a Victorian bathroom with original toilet and a small kitchen.

There is a fine hanging staircase, built at the time of conversion to a shop, but the well of the staircase has been blocked off above the street level rooms owing to shop alterations in the last 50 years. Outside the dining room is the former lift shaft for food, later replaced by some steep stairs from the kitchen.

The original shop was half the present size, the back part being Douglas Row's sight-testing room. Later on the shop was enlarged and Arthur Row's optician's room created out of an

existing office behind. Beyond is the watch and clock repair room. At the rear is the old kitchen with brick floor and old range. Through a side door is the exit to the garden. Some steps in the back wall show that there was formerly a door (now a window) into the garden from the present workroom. This would have led from the house to the original workroom at the bottom of the garden. Beyond the garden was the leasehold part of the property which gave access to Water Skellgate, sold in the 1950s by A.M. Row.

The fittings of the shop remain practically unaltered. There are old drawers under the windows, and slots showing where there were pull-put seats for the assistants. A photograph of the Severs brothers outside the shop hangs on the wall. The earliest document found relating to the history of the building is a conveyance, dated 14 June 1746, by John Charnock to Edmund Braithwaite. This refers to the property as 'formerly two messuages, cottages or tenements' owned by his grandfather, Thomas Charnock, who was a hosier, and it was presumably he who converted the two cottages into the present house.

His heir was his son, also called Thomas Charnock, a woollen draper, admitted a freeman in 1678, elected an Alderman in 1686, and Mayor in 1689-90 and 1703-4. In 1701 he was paid 'for the bellman's coate cloth 12s 3d, for making and trimming 6s 3d'. 1702 he is recorded as giving £1.1.6 towards the cost of the Obelisk. He died in 1719. One of his sons, George, a bridle cutter, was elected Alderman in 1748 and Mayor in 1750-1. He married Ellen, heiress of John Allanson, and retired to Wakefield.

The elder son, John Charnock, also a woollen draper, inherited the Market Place house. In the 1746 conveyance he is said to have lived in the 'dwelling house at Kirkgate Head, adjoining a messuage or tenement wherein Elizabeth Palliser dwelt on the west.....' John Charnock was Mayor in 1722-3 and 1733-4, and died in 1748.

By the 1746 conveyance, the new owner, for the sum of £180, was Edmund Braithwaite, apothecary and surgeon. He was admitted freeman in 1736, was made Alderman in 1743 and Mayor in 1745- 6. He died in 1748 and left the house to his wife and daughter, both named Elizabeth. The daughter Elizabeth married her cousin Christopher Braithwaite, who in a 1763 conveyance was stated to be the tenant of the house. Christopher, a mercer and woollen draper, was three times Mayor (1752-3, 1766-7 and 1779-80). He died in 1780 aged 75.

The new owners by the conveyance of 2 February 1763 were Thomas and Mary Kitchingman, for a sum of £350. They are commemorated on a floor tomb in the North Transept of the Cathedral: 'Thomas Kitchingman Esq. son of Christopher and Isabella Kitchingman, died 10 February 1793 aged 63 years. Mary, wife of the above Thomas Kitchingman, who departed this life 18 December 1822 aged 85 years'. In her will Mrs. Kitchingman left £300 to Jepson's Hospital.

On 6 April 1822 the house was sold by John Grimston and Horner Reynard, the heirs of Thomas and Mary Kitchingman, to Joseph Beevers Terry. Mr. Terry was a banker and property owner, and 42 Market Place was let to tenants. In 1851 the house was the home of Miss Anna Allanson and a conveyance of 1853 also refers to another tenant, Miss Hodgson, before Miss Allanson. In the 1851 census Miss Allanson is stated to be aged 62, a gentlewomen employing three servants.

On the death of Joseph Beevers Terry in 1853 the house was bought by James Fairburn at a public auction at the Unicorn Hotel for £830. The garden with access to Water Skellgate had a stable and coachhouse, let to Miss Allanson.

The 1861 census shows the house tenant to be Richard Blakeborough, a jeweller aged 42 with wife Jane (43) and children Richard (11), Isabella (14) and Jane Catherine (19). Richard Blakeborough stood in the Council election of 1860 but was not elected.

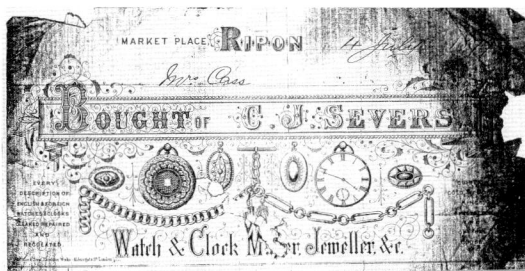

In 1871 Elizabeth Severs and family were living in the house east of the Town Hall. Her sons Thomas and Charles were fellmongers, which must have been a family business as other Severs (including John - see below) were fellmongers, woolstaplers and rug makers in nearby Wellington Street. By 1881 the tenancy of No. 42 had passed to the Severs family, the census revealing that the house was occupied by Elizabeth Severs, widow, aged 69 and a property owner, with her children Thomas (38, unmarried, and now a silversmith), Charles (30, unmarried, also now a silversmith) and Elizabeth (34 unmarried), all born in Ripon. A West Riding trade directory of 1875 gives Charles J. Severs at 42 Market Place, so the change of business and location must have been between 1871 and 1875.

A trade directory of 1927 records that 'On the North Road is a handsome drinking fountain erected and presented in 1875 by Mr John Severs'. This is now in Spa Park, and was the work of another branch of the family.

Ownership of the house passed to the Severs family when Charles Johnson Severs purchased the property on 13 August 1894 from James Fairburn of Caxton Lodge for £2000. Twenty-five years later, on 1 March 1919, Severs sold it to William Douglas Row for £2100.

Douglas Row had been apprenticed to Mr. Severs, and records had earlier referred to the jewellery business there as Row and Hill (1906, 1912) and Row and Son (1917). Douglas Row died in January 1932 and was described in the Gazette as 'the first optician to introduce modern scientific methods of eye testing to Ripon'.

William Douglas Row was succeeded by his son, Arthur Mallinson Row. The business was left to him on condition that a rent of £85 per annum was paid to his mother, Mrs. Kate Row, during her lifetime. On her death in January 1940 the premises went to Arthur M. Row who sold the leasehold land at the rear of the property in 1952.

Arthur Mallinson Row died in 1962 and was succeeded by his son David Douglas Row who took over both the optical practice and the jewellery business. In 1963 he separated the two, transferring the optics to premises in Fishergate where he practised until emigrating to Perth, Australia, in 1966 with his wife and two daughters, the business having been sold.

Meanwhile Arthur Row's widow Gladys took over the jewellery business and managed it with the help of staff and her married daughter Margaret McArdle after the latter's return from Africa. Mrs. Row died in 1991. Mrs. McArdle now runs the business with her partner David Horn and Robin Rowland.

Dorothy Sherwood

140

INDEX

◄